SOULFUL STORIES OF LOVE & EMPOWERMENT

<u>Vision One</u>
Love Heals - Stories of Love's Healing Journeys
  - Visionary: Candace Hawkshaw

<u>Vision Two</u>
Keep Calm and Live your Empowered Life
  - Visionary: Andrea Lavallee

Compiled by Anita Sechesky

LWL PUBLISHING HOUSE
Brampton, Canada

SOULFUL STORIES OF LOVE & EMPOWERMENT
– Love Heals - Stories of Love's Healing Journeys
– Keep Calm and Live Your Empowered Life

Copyright © 2017 by LWL PUBLISHING HOUSE
A division of Anita Sechesky – Living Without Limitations Inc.

All rights reserved. No part of this publication may be reproduced, distributed or transmitted in any form or by any means, including photocopying, recording, or other electronic or mechanical methods, without prior written permission of the publisher, except in the case of brief quotations embodied in critical reviews and certain other noncommercial uses permitted by copyright law. For permission requests, write to the publisher, addressed "Attention: Permissions Coordinator," at the address below.

Anita Sechesky – Living Without Limitations Inc.
lwlclienthelp@gmail.com
www.lwlpublishinghouse.com

Publisher's Note: This book is a collection of personal experiences written at the discretion of each co-author. LWL PUBLISHING HOUSE uses American English spelling as its standard. Each co-author's word usage and sentence structure have remained unaltered as much as possible to retain the authenticity of each chapter.

Book Layout © 2017 LWL PUBLISHING HOUSE

SOULFUL STORIES OF LOVE & EMPOWERMENT
– Love Heals - Stories of Love's Healing Journeys
– Keep Calm and Live Your Empowered Life

Anita Sechesky – Living Without Limitations Inc.
ISBN 978-1-988867-01-4
ASIN 1-988867-01-4

Book Cover: LWL PUBLISHING HOUSE
Inside Layout: LWL PUBLISHING HOUSE

CONTENTS

LEGAL DISCLAIMER 1

FOREWORD 3

OPENING REMARKS 7

VISION ONE 9
Love Heals - Stories of Love's Healing Journeys – Candace Hawkshaw

ACKNOWLEDGMENTS 11

INTRODUCTION 13

CHAPTER ONE 15
School of Love – Candace Hawkshaw

CHAPTER TWO 19
Angels are Watching Over Me – Mary Willemsen

CHAPTER THREE 21
Love Can Change the World – Diane Freitas

CHAPTER FOUR 23
Birth of Kale. Birth of a Mother. Birth to the Deepest Form of Love.
- Sarah Noseworthy Nickason

CHAPTER FIVE 25
The MARRIAGE House – Annette Moreland (Sanetha)

CHAPTER SIX 33
Everything is Connected – Annette Moreland (Sanetha)

CHAPTER SEVEN 43
How I Found Love through Mourning – Tara Nadia Campbell

CHAPTER EIGHT 47
Reflection – Tara Nadia Campbell

CHAPTER NINE 49
Love and Gratitude For The Future – Joey Wargachuk

CHAPTER TEN 51
Follow the Messages & Signs – Karen Phelps

CHAPTER ELEVEN 57
Wings of Love – Trina Virgin

CHAPTER TWELVE 63
The Journey of Love – Candace Hawkshaw

CHAPTER THIRTEEN 67
Love Your Scars – Danielle Hughes

CHAPTER FOURTEEN 69
Loving Light Energy of Holy Fire and the Angels – Suzanne Bertolas

CHAPTER FIFTEEN 71
Love Empathy – Natalie Friese

CHAPTER SIXTEEN 75
Musings of a Romantic Heart – Danielle Hughes

CHAPTER SEVENTEEN 79
The Reluctant Messenger – Trina Virgin

CHAPTER EIGHTEEN 83
The Healing Power of Passion – Mary Lynn Stevenson

CHAPTER NINETEEN 85
My Little Girl – Candace Hawkshaw

CONCLUSION 89

VISION TWO 91
Keep Calm and Live Your Empowered Life – Andrea Lavallee

ACKNOWLEDGMENTS 93

DEDICATION 95

INTRODUCTION 97

SECTION ONE 99
    Stories of Self-Empowerment – Andrea Lavallee

CHAPTER TWENTY 101
    Phoenix Rising – Charise Morris

EMPOWER BOOST 105
    Growing up Tina – Tina Gaisin

CHAPTER TWENTY-ONE 107
    Meditations to Empower Your Soul – Andrea Lavallee

EMPOWER BOOST 115
    Beautiful Sorrow – Charise Morris

CHAPTER TWENTY-TWO 117
    From Rags to Diamonds – Ana Marie Gonzales Agojo

EMPOWER BOOST 121
    How I Developed Self-Compassion and Learned
    to Soothe Myself…Instantly- Veronica Hislop

CHAPTER TWENTY-THREE 123
    I Am Living My Empowered Life – Andrea Lavallee

EMPOWER BOOST 129
    Who Am I? – Barbara Finlay

CHAPTER TWENTY-FOUR 131
    I Never Wanted to Give up, Ever – Andrea Lavallee

EMPOWER BOOST 135
    I See My Beauty. I Feel My Power. I Recognize My Worth. – Rose Nixon

CHAPTER TWENTY-FIVE 137
    Perseverance Is My Only Option – Janine Berridge-Paul

EMPOWER BOOST 141
How Reiki Can Help You Heal – Andrea Lavallee

CHAPTER TWENTY-SIX 145
How to Feel Free and Alive… – Lisa Berry

EMPOWER BOOST 149
Just When You Think All the Cards Are Dealt… – Lori Canlas-De Pala

CHAPTER TWENTY-SEVEN 151
Regina's Journey – Regina Neal

EMPOWER BOOST 157
Is Happiness a Myth? – Andrea Lavallee

CHAPTER TWENTY-EIGHT 159
The Little Engine That Can – Tina Gaisin

SECTION TWO 163
Stories of Being Empowered by an Individual or Community
– Andrea Lavallee

CHAPTER TWENTY-NINE 165
Embracing Life's Lessons: 10 Tips to Live a More Empowered Life. Part 1
– Andrea Lavallee

EMPOWER BOOST 169
Knowledge is Empowerment – Amna Malik

EMPOWER BOOST 171
Being One with Your Spirit – Lori Canlas-De Pala

CHAPTER THIRTY 173
Embracing Life's Lessons: 10 Tips to Live a More Empowered Life. Part 2
– Andrea Lavallee

EMPOWER BOOST 177
Divine Intervention or Law of Attraction? – Andrea Lavallee

EMPOWER BOOST 179
How the Internet Saved My Life – Lisa Berry

CHAPTER THIRTY-ONE 181
Forging the Metal – Lori Canlas-De Pala

EMPOWER BOOST 187
I Made a Promise to Myself – Andrea Lavallee

EMPOWER BOOST 189
IQ_EQ2 – Barbara Finlay

CHAPTER THIRTY-TWO 191
I Knew It Would Get Better – Laurentino Uscanga

EMPOWER BOOST 195
Money Matters – Regina Neal

EMPOWER BOOST 197
Relationship Tips – Ana Marie Gonzales Agojo

CHAPTER THIRTY-THREE 199
The Blind Spot in the Bathroom Mirror – Lisa Berry

EMPOWER BOOST 205
Thank You Mum – Janine Berridge-Paul

EMPOWER BOOST 207
The Biggest Mistake I Made in Business and How I Learned from It
– Allan Pollett

CHAPTER THIRTY-FOUR 209
Having a Positive Fertility – Andrea Lavallee

EMPOWER BOOST 213
This Wasn't Part of My Plan – Michelle Carter

EMPOWER BOOST 215
Tools to Maintain Emotional Wellness – Andrea Lavallee

CONCLUSION 217

CLOSING REMARKS 219

LEGAL DISCLAIMER

The information and content contained within this book *Soulful Stories of Love & Empowerment* does not substitute any form of professional counsel such as a Psychologist, Physician, Life Coach, or Counselor. The contents and information provided does not constitute professional or legal advice in any way, shape, or form.

All chapters are written at the *discretion* of and with the full accountability of each writer. Anita Sechesky – Living Without Limitations Inc. or LWL PUBLISHING HOUSE is not liable or responsible for any of the specific details, descriptions of people, places or things, personal interpretations, stories and experiences contained within. The Publisher is not liable for any misrepresentations, false or unknown statements, actions, or judgments made by any of the contributors or their chapter contents in this book. Each contributor is responsible for their own submissions and have shared their stories in good faith to encourage others.

Any decisions you make and the outcomes thereof are entirely your own doing. Under no circumstances can you hold the Compiler, LWL PUBLISHING HOUSE, or "Anita Sechesky – Living Without Limitations Inc." liable for any actions that you take.

You agree not to hold the Compiler, LWL PUBLISHING HOUSE, or "Anita Sechesky – Living Without Limitations Inc." liable for any loss or expense incurred by you, as a result of materials, advice, coaching or mentoring offered within.

The information offered in this book is intended to be general information with respect to general life issues. Information is offered in good faith; however, you are under no obligation to use this information.

Nothing contained in this book shall be considered legal, financial, or actuarial advice.

The author or Publisher assume no liability or responsibility to actual events or stories being portrayed.

It may introduce what a Life Coach, Counselor or Therapist may discuss with you at any given time during scheduled sessions. The advice contained herein is not meant to replace the Professional roles of a physician or any of these professions.

Soulful Stories of Love & Empowerment

FOREWORD

Thank you so much for purchasing your copy of this book. I am really curious what kind of emotions come to you when you think about the title of this publication, specifically the words "Soulful Stories of Love & Empowerment." Personally, I feel the warmth of love's energies and the strength that comes from being empowered. Stepping into a realm of beautiful possibilities evokes my spirit and I am truly excited to read more about how these true stories have shaped the very lives of those who have experienced each moment of their personal transformation and enlightened strength to become exactly who they aspired to be.

There are many journeys that await you throughout the pages and you will learn more about what our two visionaries have intended for their sections to bring to each of their readers. What's so exciting about an anthology of this nature is that it's like a double-feature at a Drive-In; you come for one really good movie and stay for the other because it has spoken to you in such an exciting way you have never thought of before. It's much like a surprise party that never gave away the element of surprise, so you truly are blessed with all the bells and whistles that come with it!

Working with Candace Hawkshaw and Andrea Lavallee has been a blessing to get to know their hearts and souls of who they are, and how powerful a message they each have to share with the world. I will not deny that there was a moment of questioning myself if we could pull it together and create a unique anthology that still gave each vision the platform they both truly deserved without diluting the intention of the message behind it. I can now say that we have done it!

The co-authors from both teams are the most amazing and beautiful souls themselves. They so graciously and courageously shared from deep within their souls. When this book title presented itself to me for this new series of "Soulful Stories" books, I knew it was the perfect fit to encapsulate all of these incredible stories.

I am very excited to introduce you to Candace and Andrea as well as their co-authors. Now I will ask you to please take a moment and appreciate who you are and the journey that has also brought you to where you are today reading this amazing book. If you have a vision or life experience that resonates with this whole book concept and what it presents, please contact me to discuss your book idea and vision. I would love to also work with you in creating your legacy in print.

When you have a vision, it becomes even more beautiful as it unfolds and develops into the finished product. This why having a supportive and professional team to collaborate with your vision is the most productive way to go. Often times, our vision must evolve to reflect the people who are also helping to bring it to life. This does not mean the original intention is of less value, it actually means it has been through a refining process to perfect it into becoming something that suits a larger audience, if that was the intention to begin with. The vision never really changes but the presentation may. Therefore, the goal is still accomplished. It has then become a multifaceted vision, enveloping all the loving energy contributed by each beautiful soul helping to fashion it, much like a diamond gemstone that reflects all of its glistening qualities, as each aspect of its valued contribution is perfected into bringing the whole vision to life from conception to birth.

Sometimes the experiences of others are where we find our greatest treasures for a life better lived. Your journey is always fascinating, but it's up to you to decide how you will grow and evolve into your most beautiful soul. By staying in constant gratitude, you can train your emotions to attract so much more abundance, joy, love, and bliss. Healing is a natural flow of these conscience behaviors when you choose to live without expectations but in appreciation of all, for all.

If you would also like to have the vision of your own anthology sponsored by LWL PUBLISHING HOUSE, (Valued at $650 CAD + HST) with you being the Compiler/Visionary, please contact:

Anita Sechesky, CEO, Founder & Publisher @ LWL PUBLISHING HOUSE or visit our website: www.lwlpublishinghouse.com

Anita Sechesky, RN, CPC, Publisher

Anita Sechesky is the Founder and CEO of Anita Sechesky - Living Without Limitations Inc. She is an RN, CPC, Best-Seller Publisher, Book Writing Mentor, Multiple International Best-Selling Author, Conference Host, Keynote Speaker, as well as a Law of Attraction and NLPP.

Anita is also the CEO, Founder, Owner, and Publisher of her company LWL PUBLISHING HOUSE.

Currently, her company has successfully branded approximately 330 International Best-Selling authors in the last four years. LWL PUBLISHING HOUSE is a division of her company, in which she offers coaching, mentoring, motivation, marketing, and of course publishing services for her clients. 2016 marked the addition of LWL KIDz and the introduction of non-fictional single author books.

Working with Anita at one of her "LWL INSPIRED TO WRITE" workshops, MasterClass, Webinars, or one-to-one support, will equip you to step out of your comfort zone fearlessly! Anita's solo book entitled "Absolutely YOU! - Overcome False Limitations & Reach Your Full Potential" was written in less than four weeks and she can teach you how to do the same! Join Anita's "Absolutely YOU!" MasterClass at: www. http://lwlpublishinghouse.com/masterclass/

Join my Private Facebook group: LIVING WITHOUT LIMITATIONS LIFESTYLE. With over 950 members, we offer exclusive prizes, co-authoring opportunities, Random Contests with FREE Publishing possibilities, "Inspired To Write" Webinar classes, and more - http://bit.ly/1TlsTSm

Please visit our Facebook page: LWL PUBLISHING HOUSE

Website: www.lwlpublishinghouse.com

Email: lwlclienthelp@gmail.com.

Join my Private Facebook group:

LIVING WITHOUT LIMITATIONS LIFESTYLE: Exclusive prizes, co-authoring opportunities and Random Contests with FREE Publishing opportunities: http://bit.ly/1TlsTSm

YouTube Channel: http://bit.ly/1VEGHew

Website: www.anitasechesky.com

LinkedIn: https://ca.linkedin.com/in/asechesky

Twitter: https://twitter.com/nursie4u

Currently, we are filling co-author opportunities for all our upcoming #Hashtag books in this series:

#Joy – The Emotion to Embrace

#Faith – The Gift that Keeps on Giving

Opening Remarks

Every once in a while, something brilliant and beautiful crosses our paths and we either choose to run alongside of it, treasure it, or allow it to move on, completely shutting it down altogether. The beauty in choosing to bring it into our lives is we get to understand and appreciate exactly what it's all about. In doing so, this enables a whole universe of opportunities to present themselves in our lives. The opposite can take place when we choose to release the best opportunities; they may never come into our lives again once we close that door. By letting go of certain blessings that life presents us, we have no one else to blame or point our fingers at any longer – we are the only ones responsible for continuing a cycle of sadness, disappointments, and ongoing negative realities.

The concept of Compiling two visions into one Compilation was never the intention of this anthology. It was a journey of understanding and patience. As things moved along from one ideal vision, it became apparent that a unique marriage had to take place. Faced with the uncertainty that the outcome would not be as originally expected, my decision to join these two beautiful visions became clear as the solution for a successful and even more beautiful reality for all involved powerfully revealed itself. Since this incredible experience, LWL PUBLSHING HOUSE now has more beautiful multi-vision books being established that will be birthed in the future. It has now become an amazing concept that we would like to proudly say was a blissful creation meant to bring so much more!

The same can be said of love and empowerment. These two very different energies always seem to balance each other out, and for the purpose of this anthology, they are a perfect complement to one another. As for my personal experience when it comes to either one of these topics, they remain highly significant in people's lives. Love will open many doors of hope, healing, growth, and even pain and heartache because of how strong of an emotion it really is. When an individual goes through a season of welcoming love into their life, many levels of awareness are brought to the surface. There is also a shedding away of many trapped emotions that may never have been explored or appreciated from previous experiences as well as damaged and unhealed feelings. Love should permit an individual to evolve into their natural process on an emotional journey of self-actualization.

Empowerment is a strong experience that many would equate to being reinforced with something powerful and significant. In order to find empowerment, one must first seek it or it may not be taken at the face value it presents itself. There are many life experiences we all walk through and if we do not remain in a state of calmness or patience, the experience itself will lose its powerful effect and we miss out on the whole point of that unique empowering moment. In fact, each one of us had very significant experiences in our lives at some point where we have seen how life shifted and recognized it for what it was. Had we not embraced that moment, we would never have benefited from its lesson and enlightenment.

This book will show you many things from the power of love and how we can find our strength in the most unlikely of places. As you read the stories from each Vision, embrace the messages they are telling you. Allow yourself the freedom to step into the beautiful awareness of what your soul is speaking and shift into who you were created to be. Once you are open to evolving into your greatest self possible, nothing is impossible within your soul.

We all sense energies whether we admit it or not, but the heavier or lighter the energies, you can be sure it will be transmuted somehow to the individual you are conversing with. Therefore, in life we need to approach all things with a sense of calmness and grace that invites the right people to come alongside of us. Whatever it is you are working on at the moment, it may need to be looked at through new eyes to capture all that it's meant to be. Don't allow frustrations or set-backs to take away the joy of what may be. Never just let go of your experiences and opportunities, re-evaluate and see what life is trying to teach you in that very moment. If we all dropped things just because it did not go according to plan, where would we be today? Life is meant to have movement and go in different directions. Therefore, plans will sometimes take a different turn in the road but still lead to the same destination if you believe strongly enough in the vision and dream of the outcome!

Vision One:

Love Heals - Stories of Love's Healing Journeys

LWL PUBLISHING HOUSE

ACKNOWLEDGMENTS

It is with gratitude and love that I share with you and acknowledge the people who stood by, supported, and loved me for who I truly am. It has been a fun journey.

Thank you to my mom, Georgina, for helping me with my writing and my editing. Thank you for believing in me and for having patience with my writing skills. Thank you for being my mom and the wise woman who taught me to always believe I can do anything. Thank you for bringing me life.

My dad, Tom. Thank you for your support, and for always asking me how I am doing with all of my books and my business.

Thank you, Sarah, my daughter, who supported me with your unconditional love. You kept me going with your wisdom and reminders of how amazing I am, helping me to come out of my comfort zone, and for listening to my "Can I do this?" Your answer is always: "Yes."

Thank you, Crystal, my daughter. You gave me inspiration and showed me different ways of looking at my life through your eyes. You spoke your truth when you thought I was going way off my path.

Thank you, Monica, my oldest daughter, who supported me and believed in me.

Thank you to my brother Bill. You are always there for me no matter how "woo woo" it sounds, and always walk beside me without judgement.

Thank you, Ginny, my sister, for supporting me through some difficult times in my life, and for helping me with this book.

Thank you to Sue and Dave, my friends for over twenty-five years. I am truly grateful for you both. Thank you for loving and accepting me for who I am, no matter how far out I sound.

Thank you, Sean and Claire, my amazing friends, for loving me unconditionally, for sharing your lives with me, for showing me love, and the power of it. Love is overflowing.

Thank you, Tammy, for inviting, encouraging, and supporting me to write in my first book. Thank you for showing me a part of myself that was hidden.

Thank you, Terry, my friend, for supporting me, even though we live miles away from each other. Thank you for loving me unconditionally.

To all my friends. I am in deep gratitude for your support in my life, and on this book project.

Thank you to all my clients and students for sharing your journeys with Reiki, sharing your experiences, and your love.

Thank you to all the co-authors who came out of their comfort zones to support me on this book project, and to share our experiences with the world.

Thank you Anita Sechesky, my publisher, for your guidance and support on this book project.

Thank you Kristine Gravelle-Rystenbil, a fellow Compiler for being a true leader in *"Ruby Red Shoes – Empowering Stories on Relationships, Intuition & Purpose,"* and for your guidance when I chose to compile this book.

Thank you to Rebecca Carrigan from Becca Blue Artistry & Design for taking some of the co-authors Bio pictures.

Thank you to all the people who I have crossed paths with, who have shared on my journey, and brought awareness to me of who I am and how I function in this life.

Candace Hawkshaw

VISION ONE
INTRODUCTION

One summer day my friend called me and said, "Hey Candace, there's a book we can write in and share our life stories." I was thrilled, but this meant coming way out of my comfort zone. "I am not a writer," I said. I thought of every excuse possible not to write in this book. Then I got my courage and decided it was time to come out and show people who I am.

Once I successfully submitted a chapter in that book, I had the opportunity to meet with the publisher. She informed me that I could be a compiler of my own anthology. Wow! I could actually gather co-authors and write about Reiki and Love in a book that would be read all over the world. It would not only have true experiences of how Love has changed people's lives, but it would also be real stories of how Love heals.

"Love Heals – Stories of Love's Healing Journeys" is filled with stories of miracles, love, and magic from all over the world that will melt your heart.

I became a Reiki Master in the late 1990's. This changed my life. It brought me greater awareness of the need for compassion and Love. I truly found my purpose in this life – to spread Love. I was shown there was more to life than working, eating, and sleeping. I began to really feel and understand Love as the most powerful energy in the universe. Love is very humbling, and flows and radiates through me. I am not the healer; the energy of Love is. I am the bridge that connects a person to the healing of Love.

Let me ask you: when your child falls and hurts themselves, what is the first thing you do? You lay your hands on them and send love. This source of healing has been around since the beginning of time.

Have an open heart, and accept the love and power you may receive from each story that you read. Please allow yourself to be open to the magic and possibilities this amazing, powerful energy of love has to offer.

I welcome you to connect with any of us in this book.

Chapter 1

School of Love
by Candace Hawkshaw

I welcome you to my healing journey in my School of Love.

I always appeared to others as this strong woman who had it all: money, looks, many friends, and blessed with amazing children and grandchildren. Little did people know of, or see, the deep feelings that I hid from everyone. I rarely showed my vulnerability, yet, I asked others to show me theirs. I discovered on my journey that the love I sought was not outside of myself, but within.

I was asked by my friend to join her writing in a book called *"Ruby Red Shoes – Empowering Stories on Relationships, Intuition & Purpose."* I came way out of my comfort zone to write and to be in the public eye sharing my story about my purpose here on Earth, which is to spread Love.

As an offering to the co-authors, the compiler gave us a gift of a hand analysis. I had a palm reading done before, but never this kind. I was super excited when it was my turn. I had my hand analysis done, and it was funny what it showed. I chuckled when I was given the report. I knew then and there that I am on a cool journey to really understand myself and love.

The report affirmed that My Life Theme and Base Skill set are:

- "School of Love" (my spiritual foundation for why I am here on Earth).

- The Heart, Love and Emotion, Emotional Mastery, Closeness and Love Matter Most ~ Relationships Are Everything ~ Mastery of Self-Love.

Your Objective is:

- Emotional Mastery – Becoming fully responsive to my own emotions / feelings and staying present with feelings no matter the content.

My life lesson is:

- "Love vs Stuffed Feelings – Emotional Authenticity Issues." I always knew deep down that my journey here was to spread love.

Since receiving my report, I have been looking into my past and present to see if I have been mastering love. In my past, I wanted everyone to love me. It saddened me when I did not feel loved in return, the way I thought I should be. Some friends only wished to be around me to access information or to get something from me. I realize now I felt needed by them, and I thought that was love.

All of my life I had thought and felt I was 'in love." All my romantic relationships ended because there was no equal love, acceptance of me for who I really was, nor was love given freely or naturally. There was manipulation, control, and expectations. I was formed into who they were, so they would, in my mind, need me, thus love me.

I loved the men in my relationships deeply, but somehow never felt the same in return. There was betrayal, secrets, manipulation, and dishonesty. The pain from these experiences led me to say, "I will never love intimately again." I energetically blocked that part of my heart from loving a man intimately ever again in fear of loss, hurt, and all the pain it would cause. I know now that I should never have said those words, and it has taken many years to reverse them.

I have learned compassion and love through Reiki, and how to move through the yucky feelings with love. Instead of hiding out, denying, blaming, rationalizing, justifying, explaining, or stuffing my feelings, I am a student of love.

I have learned to see beauty in everyone and everything. I look at nature and I am in awe of her beauty. I look at people, animals, and even physical man-made architecture seeing the beauty in it all. Have you ever been walking in the forest, felt love for no apparent reason, and love just flowed out of you and around you as you felt such joy and happiness?

My biggest realization with love is when I took Reiki. My life shifted after that. I felt such joy, love, and peace inside me. I really saw that I love everyone, no matter what. I have come to understand the difference between love, and how society defines love today. Love is not about someone needing you, and if they left, you would die. It is not about testing their loyalty, nor testing the trust you have for them. Love is without fear, judgment, expectations and is a natural flow of gratitude. Love sometimes is not spoken – some show it in other ways, such as hugs, checking in on you, saying "I miss you," or "Thank you."

When entering into any kind of relationship, whether it is romantic or friendship, I find that that I now desire to be around people who share love the same as I do. They are compatible, and they naturally reciprocate love and gratitude.

"I love you" flows out of my heart with ease, because I truly do love and I will continue to understand myself, grow, and learn in my School of Love. I see people through my heart, my whole being, and eyes with love. I love you.

I noticed it is hard for people to hear these words "I love you," especially when I have only known them for a short time. I see this often with both my students and clients. By assisting them in receiving and understanding love, I first express my gratitude, and then my love to them. Love is not purely romantic love and does not prohibit you from loving everyone and everything.

I have learned some of my lessons in love from my most cherished friends. Ours is a natural love. We don't see each often, but when we connect, it's like we've never been apart. There are no expectations or uncertainties in our love for each other. I have friends whom I have known for years. They have seen me at my worst, and at my best. No matter what, they love me for me, and I love them. In a relationship of any kind, love flows naturally, without competitiveness or jealousy, but just pure unconditional love for one another.

The innocence of my grandchildren has shown me the most love of all. They are pure divine beings, and I have witnessed the love and joy they bring to so many people. For example, when walking down the street, or in a store, people see them and light up because these children are balls of pure love.

I feel that I've come a long way in understanding love, and how I allow it to flow in my life through my experiences and Reiki lifestyle. My journey with love has shown me that love flows through me and around me in all time, space, and dimension; it is infinite. I have a better understanding of who I am and look forward to sharing my experiences so others may understand love. Learning to love myself has brought awareness of the fears I had about speaking my true feelings regarding the fear of loss and judgment. I now know that standing in my authentic self and expressing my feelings is freeing and allows me to love myself completely.

The strongest flow of love through Reiki is when you truly understand that love is not validating you, giving you what you want, or sympathizing with the person. It is compassion, caring, having gratitude, and knowing that each person is a Divine Being. Love is the highest energy in the Universe, love can heal, and Reiki is Love.

Candace Hawkshaw is a certified Holy Fire II Reiki Master, a teacher, a healer, and a mentor. She is certified in many other complementary healing modalities, and is the bridge that will connect your Soul and Spirit to the Universal Source. Candace is a weaver of Love, who will assist you on your journey to remember who you are and your purpose!! Her business is called Know Thyself. She is an international teacher. Candace has written her stories in three books: The Ruby Red Shoes - Empowering Stories on Relationships, Intuition & Purpose, Living Without Limitations - Vision Quest, & #Peace - A New Perspective of Hope.

http://www.know-thyself.ca

https://www.facebook.com/candacenhawkshaw/

Chapter 2

Angels are Watching Over Me
by Mary Willemsen

My husband and I were getting organized to leave on vacation within the next few days. We were driving to Maine to enjoy being near the ocean, swimming, relaxing, reading, and eating copious quantities of fresh seafood right off the boat. We had just undergone a major bathroom renovation that took longer than expected due to floor tiles being back ordered for five weeks and then another three weeks. It had been a rather stressful time for us with the house in disarray for so long. The bathroom was finally finished and it looked gorgeous! The bills were paid. We could now relax and enjoy life. We were ready for our vacation.

While checking the mail, my husband noticed a letter from our vehicle's manufacturer. There was a recall notice for our one and only car. There was a problem with the passenger side airbag. Considering our upcoming trip, I said to my husband, "I am going to call the nearest dealership and have this recall taken care of before we leave."

I contacted the dealership and was told there was not one, but two recall notices for our vehicle. There was an ignition problem as well. I asked if I could book an appointment for the following day for both recalls, and was told, "We do not yet have the part for the passenger airbag recall." The part would be coming in from the U.S. and would take 7-10 business days to arrive. I replied, "I don't have time to wait for a part as we were going on vacation – a driving vacation to the States." I asked, "Since we are traveling to the U.S., could we have this service done there?" "Of course," I was told. "Anywhere there is a dealership. Although I would advise getting the ignition recall serviced now." "OK," I said and made an appointment for the following day.

Since we were heading to Maine, I checked to see if there was a dealership in the area we were vacationing near. Yes, I found one! But, my husband said, "I am not spending my vacation without a car." I thought, "Well I am sure everything will be fine. I work with the Angels every day. I am an Angel Messenger. I will just offer this situation to the Divine and trust we will have a safe trip, knowing the car recall will be serviced upon our return."

Easy to say...easy to try to fix it myself? What if my Angels aren't listening? Shall I take matters into my own hands? Should I call a dealership across the U.S. border and see if they have the recall part available for the airbag? I could drive across the border, have the car serviced before our trip next week, and not have to worry about the defective passenger airbag blowing up and injuring me while on vacation. Or...I could ask the Angels to handle this problem. The Angels protect me always and the defective airbag problem hasn't hurt me so far.

The next day, a couple of hours had passed since my husband left to have the car serviced. I was wondering why it was taking him so long to return home. I wondered where he could be.

I checked the telephone and saw that he had left a message. He was still at the dealership. It seems the service center did indeed have the parts available for the two recalls on our car. They were both being installed that day! I sighed a breath of relief. A Miracle! No worries concerning car problems for our upcoming trip. I could rest and relax while enjoying the calm of the ocean.

Once I let go and let the Divine handle the problem, all was taken care of immediately. Trust the Divine to see to your needs. All you have to do is ask and be grateful.

Mary Willemsen is a Reiki Master, an Angel Messenger, an Intuitive Reader, and a Fairyologist. Although Mary works from her Reiki studio in Ottawa, Ontario, she also offers Distance Healing to clients all over the world. Mary enjoys bringing the Angels' love and light to the world while helping her clients unleash their inner strength.

www.reikirelaxation.ca

Chapter 3

Love Can Change the World
by Diane Freitas

For years, it seems I have never been accepted by family. When I had a dream, no one took me for real. My thoughts on life were crazy. My feelings of love, at times, were wrong. All I said and did and every one of my choices were all wrong. It was when my father passed away that something happened...something I can't describe. My family was already at war, but that day I felt such peace within. Yet, my whole family, brothers and sisters, fell apart. I felt lonely. My husband and children were now all that I had. I thought I knew love and forgiveness, but it wasn't till I began my journey with Reiki that I truly found out what love really is, how it makes you feel, and how it all works. I now have an understanding of this beautiful love and know how it truly feels. It's so deep.

My husband and I decided to sell our home, quit our jobs, and take a chance. We wanted to make changes to have less stress and to view our thoughts in a more positive way. For me, I wanted to take more time to sit and relax with no worries. If it was possible, I would stay on top of a mountain and just meditate. I have accomplished my goal to live differently, without things that have no real meaning. I wanted my children to see that we don't need materials to make us feel love, and that you can do anything you choose to do.

Many people couldn't understand, but we took a chance, and it was the best move we ever made. Our home now has more strength, more love. This love is with me every second of every day – from the moment I wake up, right through to when I go to sleep. I see everything around me. I breathe all of nature so vividly. Everything around us has purpose. It seems to speak to my heart and soul. All that sadness has disappeared. A weight has been lifted off my shoulders. This is the happiest I have ever been. My husband and children also see it. To actually know and feel the warmth of everything we see and touch, and to live in a positive way with just pure love, a better understanding of people and nature, even water, brings so much to my heart and my soul. It is a Love so powerful it can change the world.

Diane Freitas is a Usui/Holy Fire II Reiki Master. She also carries her love for people as she assists with the elderly by caring for them with love and compassion. In her near future, Diane will be dedicating her services in her own space.

Reiki Revive Facebook

Chapter 4

Birth of Kale. Birth of a Mother. Birth to the Deepest Form of Love.

by Sarah Noseworthy Nickason

How does love change your world? Well it happened to me in just about six hours.

Until the moment I held Kale to my breast, I thought I understood Love. Oh yes, I had it all figured out. I had the love of Spirit in my heart, the love of my family, the love of a man. But six hours can change a person, and change her entire life.

Like a butterfly emerging from a chrysalis, it will open your heart, your body, and your soul in such a way that you become a new person.

It was April 13th, 2008 and my sacred body was ready to give birth.

There was no doubt about it. I could feel the deep surges and with each breath I took, I was transforming. Light was entering my body and exposing past trauma that I had suffered. Surges reached deep into those dark places that I did not want to enter, in fear of feeling helpless again, and out of control – but there was no escape. The light had to enter me, and my past had to be expressed. It had to be found and reclaimed.

The emotions stored in my body, where memories were kept, were touched, tightened, relaxed, and healed again and again, moved like waves with my child coming into the world. Each ebb and flow was teaching me that it's okay to be reborn, to push through to the other side.

And as I pushed through, I was allowing surrender to take place, opening a pathway for transformation.

I was changing. I was collecting all the pieces of myself, gathering them, holding them tight and weaving myself back together. No more forgetting. No more hiding.

To bring this child, this Soul into the world, I had to be whole. I had to embrace all my joys, all the hurt I was repressing deep within. What was fear and pain became love and understanding.

A young maiden becomes a Mother

I felt different, like a warrior Goddess who is strong and powerful, a moment of perfection.

With a deep breath, my body pushes one last time. Out comes this little baby boy, this miracle.

The entire universe that was once placed in my womb is now resting on my chest. It has name, a life, and is in my care.

Love now takes on a new understanding. With Love reflecting through the eyes of my child, something awakens within me – a revelation...it is Unconditional Love.

Endless, True, Perfect Love. Raw and Glorious.

Now as I have journeyed onward (nine years and two more babies later), I have come to realize that my children have chosen me, and I have chosen them. We have been called together into this wonderful challenging life, our Souls entwined, graced with the beautiful gift of unconditional LOVE.

Sarah Noseworthy Nickason is married and a mother. She is a Healer, a nature lover, a Doula, and a peaceful person. Family is her most favorite thing. Sarah is a Holy Fire II Reiki Master Teacher, loves to teach children Reiki, and is a Complimentary Care practitioner.

Chapter 5

The MARRIAGE House

by Annette Moreland (Sanetha)

There are no coincidences – you have been asking for a sign and guidance, and now you are reading this. Expect a healing to occur.

This chapter is for anyone who is struggling with one-self, relationships and/or marriage. There is a reason for everything and you are going to be okay.

Disclaimer

I AM not a marriage counselor nor AM I a therapist. In fact, I have no official documented educational credentials (at least not in this lifetime) what-so-ever to suggest that I can help you or anybody else to live a long and happy marriage and/or healing from deep wounds, a broken heart, or in the search for answers to finding the perfect marriage and/or partner.

Claimer

However, I have consulted with my spirit team in choosing a topic for this chapter. A topic that would help you now reading this, to understand, come to terms with, assist in healing, and move forward on your journey here with or without a "marriage house." You too have been guided to read this by your spirit team. LOVE works in the most mysterious ways and you should consider this chapter to be from the "Angel of Marriage."

It should also be understood that I have been known to communicate with spirit in matters such as this and more. When I discovered who I was in my previous life, less than five months before entering this one, my spirit team guided me step by step, word for word, to write my first book about past lives, reincarnation, and the "junk/dormant" DNA we all have access to when we do the work.

But of course, on the human side of me it could be said I have earned several medals in the subject of MARRIAGE and therefore deserve an honoree degree! After all, I do know a thing or two about marriage because I have had many lifetime relationship and marriage experiences tucked away in my DNA.

No two marriages are the same – I am not you and you are not me. However, we can follow the same blueprint and create our Marriage House how we see fit. LOVE THYSELF FIRST.

But more importantly in this lifetime right here in the now, I am creating brand new life experiences, while at the same time being able to access my dormant DNA to assist me to have more love and more joy in this life! In this lifetime, I have walked and sometimes ran, skipped, climbed, swam, and drowned, only to come up gasping for breath I then discovered I was stronger, wiser, and more loving than ever each time during <u>our forty-three years</u> and counting in our Marriage House.

In writing this chapter, it is my intent that I bring to you an opening to a much larger clearing, which I hope will bring a profound enlightening and understanding of WHY things had to be the way it was or is. Once acknowledged by you, it is also my intent to help guide you to accepting your journey and preparing you for your inner renovations.

EVERYTHING IS CONNECTED!

The Energy of Love

In this life, I have been carried home, tickled, and healed by ANGELS; I have been contacted by phone, in my dreams, and in my visions by ANGELS; I have been called an ANGEL; I have seen the ANGELS come to take my father to his place in the sky; and now I KNOW our son Michael walks with ANGELS as an angelic guide.

Where Does Love Come From?

What if we understood that LOVE was all around us, and that real LOVE has no conditions? Why do we look for love in all the wrong places? Why is it so difficult for some to receive love – or to give love? Why does LOVE come with overwhelming feelings of happiness and sadness – even HURT?

Where to Begin

Always begin everything with what is going on right now for you at this very moment in time. Ask yourself, what is it that I need to know right now? Be open to receiving the information of love and light that will gently flow down the stream as if by magic someone or something has a direct link to your thoughts, your dreams, and your feelings. Know that this is real. You are never alone. Remember to ask your guides and angels whenever you need help.

For me at this very moment in time as I write these notes to you, I am sitting in our two-bedroom apartment in Connecticut, USA. I just got back from our five-day trip to Ontario, Canada, where we took possession of our newest older home as we prepare for our pre-retirement back to our hometown. In this great house lived a family – the same family for sixty years. This house was loved and cared for by its owners, but never updated in all those years. The furniture and décor remained the same – never changing.

The house sits on a beautiful treed and manicured half-acre lot. The house is a super solid built front to back split home with an added breezeway (once a carport) and a two-car garage. Why AM I telling you this? That is the question I just asked my angels.

AND THE ANGELS SAID

"Renovations required! Just like a well-built house, even well maintained, loved, and cared for, changes and updates need to be made to keep in pace with the new energy. NEW LIFE and TRANSFORMATION are the keys for this house, your life, and your marriage too. Out with the old energy and in with the new!"

The Soul Knows

Change is an energy that requires everything associated with it to change. What if you and your life stayed to same day in and day out? What if everything around you was changing and you did not allow for change or want any changes? The world will move with or without you and it will become more difficult to navigate in the old energy. Then suddenly you will say, "When did all that change?" Imagine if one of you in the marriage house changes and the other one does NOT?

This doesn't mean you have failed in marriage. It just means the energy changed the union of the marriage. One becomes two and separation is the new. You go your way and they go their way – yet sometimes remaining in the same house!

We are programed to complete the next life lesson. The soul knows change is always good – even when it feels bad.

Yesterday while making the ten or eleven hour-long drive from Ontario, Canada to Connecticut, USA, as I have done so many times before with my husband, I received a message from my very dear friend Candace asking me to help her write a few more short chapters to complete this book. So, just like an angel I replied. Could it be that you have been asking for help in this area of your life and the angels knew you would be reading this? Could it be that they knew I would be writing about this too?

NEVER DOUBT A MIRACLE!

My husband was asked by his Canadian employer many years ago to go to Connecticut to help a sister company for three weeks. That was thirteen years ago…sigh. We had been married already for nearly thirty years at that time. He consulted with me and my immediate reaction was, "GO FOR IT!" I have always believed that everything is put on our path for a reason and that when opportunity knocks, we should at least open the door. Once the door is open we can see what is inside. If we don't like what we see, we can leave quietly and shut the door. Perhaps this door or another door will show up some other time.

There is no right way and there is no wrong way. If you don't do it now, then maybe you will later or maybe never. You might do it in this lifetime or maybe you will do it in another lifetime. Your guides and angels will still love you no matter what you do.

The moral of this part of the story is that when in a marriage, it does take two to make decisions that affect both parties – being in agreement, in alignment with each other.

If my husband had come home and said to me, "I'm going to Connecticut for three weeks for my company to help their sister company," and for some reason I wasn't in agreement and he went anyway, then the story of our "MARRIAGE" would now be in turmoil. I might not like the color of the walls or the size of the rooms in our "marriage house." If he wasn't married to me or anybody else then the decision would of course be his alone to make.

Now, I know that may seem simple to you and you are saying right now, "Well Sanetha, I know that already, and I am not stupid!"

My reply would be, "But did you know that most people in marriages today think they alone should be making decisions for the entire family?

In fact, most people while growing up, had loud heated discussions, with their parents, while using words like "IT'S MY LIFE" and "I WILL LIVE MY LIFE HOW I WANT TO!" It is your life and you should live your life how you want to live it. However, when others are in your life and a "MARRIAGE" exists, then one must consider the other person or persons whose lives will be affected/changed.

Change is energy – *energy constantly changes* – *when one cannot flow with the current of that energy, one will struggle with the change. This will force one to flow down another stream where the flow of the energy feels much lighter. This is perfectly okay. You are following your heart and your soul.*

MARRIAGE MEANS YOU ARE ONE – SAME VIBRATION

The Definition of Marriage

"Marriage is a community, or communion, or union of life. Through it, the spouses reciprocally give themselves to each other, sharing a common life. This sharing occurs at all the various levels of human life: physical, financial, emotional, moral, intellectual, and spiritual. The comprehensiveness of this sharing makes marital love the deepest sort of friendship." Quote from one of ten key features of the definition of marriage: http://www.thepublicdiscourse.com/2015/07/15331/

Does marriage require a piece of paper? Many people have chosen to not have a piece of paper to be together. It is a beautiful thing when two people can come to together in union, giving themselves to each other without having a piece of paper to make if official. It's not like buying a house, is it?

The Marriage House is built on a solid foundation of love and trust with two people who are compelled to be together as one. Sometimes the house needs renovating to allow for the changes in the energies created by the marriage.

Marriage is honor, trust, compassion, and unconditional love between two people. It is sacred. It can last a lifetime or it may not. People come and go into our lives for many different reasons and sometimes they are short-lived. Marriage is for better or worse, for sickness and in health. Marriage is to the day in death we part. Is that why people say when the marriage ended, it was worse than death?

When one person in the union of marriage changes and the other one does not – the marriage house breaks up. Some walls may need to be torn down and rebuilt from the bottom up to save the "Marriage House."

How to Become One with Your Partner in Marriage

I remember the day we got married. The minister who performed the ceremony said we needed to be honest and fully communicate at all times to ensure a healthy marriage. He said if I cooked my husband eggs and the eggs were not cooked the way he liked them, then he should speak up in a loving way and tell me how he liked his eggs. If he continued to eat the eggs he did not like, this negative energy might build up inside.

I know for certain that my marriage has been healthy because of the little things we do for each other that shows we care. For example, I get up every day to make his coffee and his lunch even when I am not going out anywhere. We always hug and kiss each other when one of us leaves the house and when we go to bed at night. This is how we maintain our marriage house. This does not mean you should too. You have other ideas that work well for you.

There are many things I wish we would do together. There are many things we do together which I wish we would NOT do. We don't always like the same movies or restaurants but we are willing to give and take. I usually get my way though. LOL.

Spirituality Matters – The Journey of the SOUL

How we experience and accept our feelings is all part of your unique being as a spiritual being having another glorious human experience.

Before we are born – before our soul transitions into a body, our soul family, our guides, and our angels who have been with us many times in many forms and other lifetimes are there to send us off. We are fully aware that upon entering the earth plane that we will be separated from our divine family as the veil comes down upon our delivery.

Each of us has created a plan with our beloveds which was all planned and agreed upon before our incarnation. We created a plan with a list of possibilities and probabilities that would most likely trigger our soul to search for answers to quench our thirsty questions deep within our souls.

We are all born with the most powerful energy in the universe, unconditional LOVE – it never leaves any of us. It simply gets clogged up, reprogrammed with conditions leaving us heavy with debris created by our own life experiences and often other people's stuff.

Is it time to clean up your personal house? Each of us has our own stuff to clean up that nobody can do for us. If you want to live in the "Marriage House" or any other house, then each will need to get rid of all the debris and begin the renovations within.

HAPPY RENOVATIONS and TRANSFORMATION!

SANETHA (Annette Moreland) is an inspirational & transformational spiritual and intuitive Psychic Medium, Healer, Author, Guide and Speaker, INSPIRING OTHERS TO FIND THE GOD INSIDE. SANETHA – is the name given to her by her by a team of angels and guides during the writing of her first book. She is also known in this lifetime as Annette Renee Moreland, owner of SANETHA'S SOULGENIC HEALING SOULUTIONS.

www.sanetha.com

Chapter 6

Everything is Connected

by Annette Moreland (Sanetha)

I *Feel Therefore I AM* – **Sanetha**

"Without a question there are no answers" – Sanetha (Annette Moreland)

Feelings are the most powerful force in the Universe. Compassion is the force that connects everything to the Universe – into infinity.

When you cry, all of you cry. When you laugh, all of you laugh. When you release negativity, all of you release negativity. When you feel love, all of you feel love. When you connect, all of you connect.

Imagine now all of us feeling LOVE at the same time uniting as "ONE," creating "World Peace." You are connected to everything, connected to "All That Is" – The Creator.

If you want to change something in the world, become the change you wish to see – fill up your heart with compassion and unconditional LOVE, and then happily send it out into the Universe like a dove delivering peace and good will to all.

We are connected to our source, which is the Creator God. We are all part of God; we originated as God-sparks created by "Source."

Everything?

Yes, everything!

You might be thinking at this moment, no way can I be connected to that person you just heard about on the news practically on the other side of the world, who just murdered someone in their own family. Remember Hitler?

Or how about a famous actor or singer which you adore who you have never met let alone had an opportunity to be anywhere near them? Who do you adore?

You are driving down the highway and someone is driving a car much slower than you in the passing lane and weaving in and out of the lines. After some time, you manage to get around him but not without staring him down.

Do you realize what you just did? I know at that moment you didn't realize that you just sent a very negative energy onto someone. But even more importantly, you might not have realized to what extent that negative energy will carry. Did you know that what you put out energetically will come right back at you? Also, when we react in a negative way, we are actually increasing the size of that negative energy. We are all doing this unconsciously without giving it a second thought. This happens too easily because we are programmed to react back that way. We can change this with some simple reprogramming.

Thoughts are most certainly energy too! You have heard about this many times before. Thoughts become things and when we change our thoughts we can create a better life for ourselves and for the entire world. But it goes much further than that. Our thoughts are carried throughout the entire Universe! Seriously speaking, there are many universes connected… Everything is connected.

Currently there are so many huge events taking place on our earth that have been causing an enormous amount of chaos. It doesn't matter where you live on this earth, everyone on the planet and off this planet are being affected by the energy that is out there. At this moment in our history things are about to change for the greater good of all of us.

For example, the new President of the United States just got elected and the emotions are so mixed causing division within countries, states, parties, communities, families, and friendships everywhere. Something very interesting indeed is how in the midst of all the chaos, people are coming together, standing up, and protecting each other. Sanctuary cities, churches, schools, and other places are popping up all over the United States. People are joining in standing together holding the light with UNCONDITIONAL

LOVE for the illegal immigrants who fear deportation back to Mexico. Something is happening here my friends. I know it is because of you and, because of me. We are doing this together. Everything is connected!

The former leader of Cuba just died at the age of ninety. While many celebrate FREEDOM in the streets around the world, many others praise his leadership.

Even at death, we are creating an energy that is connected to everything. I am seeing the energy clearly now, where one must divide to create something new over there. Perhaps more on this in another book.

This is an important awareness because many of you reading this have been associated with the loss of someone or something that you know too familiar. Division is needed to balance a negative or a positive. Really? As if this wasn't enough grief to deal with, outcome unforeseen and sometimes foreseen energies that make life twice as unbearable! There is a reason for everything and again everything is connected.

For months on end, people from Standing Rock in North Dakota have created a protest against a pipeline going through their sacred land and water. There are people showing up from all over the world in person and in social media to support them. I am proud to be one of them in spirit. There have been worldwide virtual and in person meditations and healing ceremonies. Wait a minute, are we coming together as a society, standing up for each other? Social media is a huge and growing energy and, yes of course it is connected to everything. It has connected us to everybody and everything. As of December 4th, 2016, the American government backed down and won't allow the pipeline easement onto this territory.

All of these events and more are causing chaos. Chaos is a huge energy in constant change, as is all energy. Chaos however, is moving faster and growing faster than most other forms of energy because basically it is on fire! Eventually, the fire will go out when there is nothing left to burn and/or when other forms of energy are applied to put the fire out. Things always get bad, before they get better. While you are waiting, you might as well start creating how you would like to see your future, our future together. We do have a choice as we all have free will and choice.

Simply stated, a good thing to remember is that whenever you feel the need to react, please figure out first what you want to create because the tools, materials, and love you use, will impact your creations. Beautiful, joyful, loving new beginnings are in the air! We can all learn to change a negative into a positive.

Losing Loved Ones

Like you, I have lost many loved ones. My father-in-law, sister-in-law, and brother-in-law all passed in the early years. I had grandparents in Holland who passed which I had never been connected to physically because I had never met them. I still feel their presence.

Then my father and my mother both passed years later. It was my friend Donna who passed so unexpectedly followed by her first husband six months later that really had me searching for more. My children witnessed the loss of their very young friends and I could not have ever imagined at that time the thought of losing my own child. There is no pain that I know greater than the loss of a child.

This huge loss came in the midst of writing a book about the great invisible spirit! I did not know why this was happening to me or did I? I was so very sad and still have days of deep sadness. I am a spiritual being living in a human body who feels all of the human emotions just like everyone else does. Another devastating twist in my life that would squeeze me until there was no more, nothing left except his spirit who became my newest guide. My dear beloved Michael helped me finish the book and now works with me whenever I connect to his and other higher vibrations. They are also connecting to me when I am accessing the healing frequencies, and the information is downloaded to me for angel and mediumship readings. Everything is connected.

I was connected and talking to my spirit guides and angels at a very young age. When I was almost five years old, I walked away from my home in search of GOD because I needed him to fix (heal) my mother who was in a full body cast from an operation she had. On three occasions, a man (the same man) carried me home as he found me on the roadside sick from the heat and exhaustion. I believed him to be the father, the holy man, God the almighty.

Often I would ask my mother who that man was. Every single time she replied, "I don't know honey." I am not sure if she knew or if she was simply embarrassed that I managed to walk away from home so many times.

The beginnings of the book showed up in 2009 as if on cue when I was shown who I was in my previous lifetime, less than five months between lives. I was not given this information through any past life regression sessions – however, I do believe this is most certainly a very POSITVE avenue for anyone seeking to check it out. My discovery was pure happenstance – divine guidance. I had always believed in past lives and reincarnation but I was not interested in the subject past that knowing. Upon this discovery, I began to reach for the heavy-duty tools needed to wrap my head around this knowing.

It took eighteen months of research, and soul searching, before I was guided by my spirit team, to write the very controversial book about past lives, reincarnation with a BIG surprise about our DNA. It is dedicated to our beloved Michael, our oldest son who passed suddenly during the writing of the book. Everything is connected.

"Without a question, there are no answers." Sanetha

I was well on my way – seeking the answers to the questions, which weighed heavily on my mind. These were the same questions that were on the minds of everyone. WHO AM I? WHERE DID I COME FROM? WHY AM I HERE? WHERE AM I GOING?

"Each question presented an answer leading me to another question." Sanetha

During this massive awakening prior to my past lives and the writing of the book, I was also guided to become a Level III Reconnective Healing Practitioner. I had not yet taken the training when my mother began to run out of oil. This was not the first time but it would be the last time I would go to the garden to ask Arch Angel Michael for more oil for my mother. I was able to assist her with the pain she had suffered with all of those years but now it was time to let go of her body and return to spirit form. It was during her transition, the doves appeared in my vision showing me that peace was coming to all.

While on this path, I started to access more of the frequencies, all connected to the original frequency or you might say a different frequency / energy which no longer suited the description of "reconnective healing" and therefore the need to create my own healing modality and, expand the process became evident to all of us.

I would recommend my good friend and soul sister, Candace Hawkshaw of Soaring Spirits, a great healer who also teaches Reiki. She is also the one who invited me to share my stories in this book. We have connected on many levels, in this lifetime and other lifetime before.

...Everything is Connected.

During the healing sessions of some of my clients, I began to give them detailed messages. These messages came from a higher place. They did not come from my earthly education in this lifetime. I began to read souls, allowing healings to occur at the soul level, and I had no idea where the information was coming from. I only knew that it was appropriate to give them the information and to also tell my clients at the end of the session that I had no idea where the information was coming from. It was up to them to decide what to do with this information. Discernment is extremely important for everyone to make the best choices at any given time. I was very clear stating that I had no medical background whatsoever in this lifetime.

Shortly thereafter, I also started to feel the presence of incarnate souls and began giving messages from heaven to my clients receiving a healing session. All of this eventually became my own healing modality. I don't teach this modality simply because it is my own brand, created with the tools I reached for, and the frequencies accessed that makes this one of a kind and unique to me. You can have one unique to you also. Everything is connected.

I offer spiritual guidance, healing sessions, angel and mediumship readings, which have all been created to help you find your way on this journey here – however, ultimately you are your own creator. You could say that I am one of the tools you have found on your path. What we create merges with, and is connected to all of creation. Everything is connected.

We are all unique spiritual beings yet we are all inter-connected. You simply take the basic tools and add more to create your own uniqueness. The same can be said if you were an artist, singer, songwriter, actor, scientist, or angel. You get my point here I think. You take your point, add my point, and then add other points along the way. Forever, you are changing up your creations to be better than ever.

Why Is This Happening to Me?

"When darkness falls upon us, it is our spirit that seeks the light. We are so much more than our bodies." **Sanetha**

We are all moving about our lives with the tools we are given, and we use these tools on a daily basis. These tools are given to us from our families, friends, education, and religious institutions. These tools have been passed down from generation to generation and modified to keep in alignment with changing times. Some of us stick with the basic tools everyone else is using – staying pretty close to the sidewalk where the majority of souls are walking.

We also possess several tools that may seem to be "out of reach" and/or out of sight. These tools came with you. They are part of you and nothing can ever take them away from you. They are connected to you and me – they are connected to everything!

These tools are hidden treasures – they are our gifts and abilities available to us, tucked away ready for our use whenever the need or desire arises. We choose when and how to use these tools. Unexpected situations in our lives show up, those unpleasant and hurtful things that "happen to us" are like keys that show up to open the next door as we begin to search for the answers to the questions that are on our minds: *"Why is this happening to me?"*

"Without the pain, there is no gain…" Things happen to us so that we will move with the flow of the energy. If we choose the path of least resistance, we will find our way with grace and ease. Just breathe…everything is connected.

It's a journey, a soul journey guiding us to come to terms and to understand why the things had to be this way. No two paths are the same, no two tools are the same, and no two doors are the same. The only thing that is the same is what we are all trying to do, and where we are all trying to go, together, connected to each other and everything.

Our tools open doors, giving us opportunities to receive and open the abundance of LOVE connecting us to all that is – you and me and everything in-between.

When darkness falls upon us, it is our spirit that seeks the light. We are so much more than our bodies. It is in our darkest hours we are able to go to that place within where we may not have previously been willing to go before. It is there, where we are able to re-connect and see that little light inside. When you find you, you will find me there too. We are one; we are connected.

When life stuff happens to us, it forces us to "reach" beyond the tools we possess. We feel more – as our hearts open more, and the need to search for more widens. These tools have been in safe keeping, hidden until we choose to receive them. Also know that there is no right and no wrong way. It is your choice when and if you do at all. Your angels and guides are always there for you and will never leave you. They can only help you when you ask.

Whatever is happening to you is also "happening to me" because we are all connected. I could not have ever imagined previous to the pain, suffering, heartbreak, depression, illness, and loss of my oldest child what was "happening to me" would have presented sacred, hidden treasures that would unlock the doorways to heaven.

You too have hidden treasures for your use only. I am able to use my tools to help you find yours. I can also use my tools to help you learn how to navigate and use your tools. When I help myself, I am also helping you – when I help you, I am also helping myself. When I shine my light and my love – more light and love shows up in the universe.

These very special tools, selected by each of us individually will reveal hidden gifts and abilities made available to us so that we can move through the situations happening in our lives with grace and ease. Some will choose the tools that open the gifts – some will not. It is up to each individual to make the choices. In many cases we ignore and/or refuse the gifts because our soul has not yet learned or completed the lesson we needed to move into the higher vibrations of our lives. That is okay. The healing begins now…

GOD Is Everywhere

We are all connected to each other, yet we are all very unique individuals feeling separate, sensing and seeking connections throughout our lifetime. We are driven by the forces within to find the "god" inside.

Inside and out of our human bodies are an unlimited number of universes all connected and working together. We are the soul creators – created by our creator "GOD".

We together are the light and the dark, the right and the wrong, the love and the hate. We are everything – we are god-like. I AM you; I AM me too. What I see in you, I also see in me.

Soul Growth – Expansion

The choice of a life of hardships is a way to learn and know what joy and happiness are. We must experience both the negative and positive in our lives to bring balance to our soul and the souls of others. The choices we make influence many other souls who also need to experience certain events in their life.

Your thoughts become things. What you project into the Universe will return to you like looking through a mirror. An energy that is out of balance will seek a path to become balanced, aligned, and whole again. The process and the passages are different for everyone and everything because no two energies are the same.

EVERYTHING IS ENERGY! EVERYTHING IS CONNECTED!

LOVE is a mighty warrior, and when applied in its purest form, will conquer all. Time to celebrate and let go of anything that is holding you back from who you really are—follow your heart.

"Thy kingdom come, Thy will be done in earth, as it is in heaven." Matthew 6:10 (KJV)

SANETHA (Annette Moreland) is an inspirational & transformational spiritual and intuitive Psychic Medium, Healer, Author, Guide and Speaker, INSPIRING OTHERS TO FIND THE GOD INSIDE. SANETHA – is the name given to her by her by a team of angels and guides during the writing of her first book. She is also known in this lifetime as Annette Renee Moreland, owner of SANETHA'S SOULGENIC HEALING SOULUTIONS.

www.sanetha.com

Chapter 7

How I Found Love through Mourning

by Tara Nadia Campbell

When we meet real tragedy in life, we can react in two ways – either by losing hope and falling into self-destructive habits or by using the challenge to find our inner strength. Dalai Lama

Two of the most life-changing moments of my life were when my parents died. I look back now and think about how lucky I was to have had their love and support, even after they were gone. This is a peek into my journey and how love has given me the coping skills to push through the darkness and walk towards love.

I was six years old when I was told my dad wasn't coming home again. I don't remember much about him, but I do remember that my little hand could only grasp his finger and I remember his smile. I was told that he was very strong – he was a power lifter when he was young and my mom would brag that he could lift the back end of a car up off the ground. He loved to dance and he loved his family. One night, my dad was working the strike line at the Mill, but he didn't come home afterwards. I remember at first my mom was mad, but then her anger turned to worry. I remember being confused. He often worked the night shift and I wouldn't see him for days. I was playing across the street at a friend's when the police pulled up to our house. I was sure they had found my dad safe and that he would be coming home soon. I ran across the street and when I got to the front door the excitement and smile fell from my face. Something was wrong. My mom pulled me to her side and held me tight before closing the door. The next few weeks were a blur of visitors and family coming from Calgary, Ontario and England. I only remember my mom crying a few times during this time. I was scared and uncertain, but my mom shared a story with me that would help me throughout my life. She told me what her mother said to her when she was young and afraid about death. You see, I never met my grandma as she was very sick and died when my mom was a teenager. One time when she was in the hospital she told my mom, "You don't have to be afraid of death anymore. It is not scary, it is peaceful and I am no longer afraid." Because my mom was so reassured by her mother, I believed her and I carried that story with me thinking of it often and giving me strength in times of fear.

Around this time, I had a recurring dream. I was floating above the house and the front door would not stay closed. It was swinging back and forth and my mom was trying to figure out why the door wouldn't stay shut. I could hear laughter in the background and I was terrified. I was then back in my bed and I was afraid to move because there were hands reaching for me and if I moved or screamed, I just knew that they would get to me. I believe that this was my fear that my dad was no longer there to protect us. We were alone. I used to see my dad from time to time after that. One particular memory was me walking through the park holding his hand. He was smiling down at me and I felt safe and warm again, and I knew that this energy was love. I have felt this energy from time to time in the thirty-two years since he has been gone. Usually when I feel scared or unsure, I feel comforted knowing that he is holding my hand and smiling down at me.

My mom, my sisters, and I became very close as I grew up. I am not sure if it was because of our loss, but we only had each other. My sisters and I fought like crazy as sisters do, but my mom would say, "You are lucky to have a sister." And she was right – sisters are you first friends. My mom and sisters are my biggest cheerleaders and an ear when I need to work out my thoughts. They each have taught me so much about life and love. My favorite thing about my mom is that when she looked at you, she saw you.

My mom did not judge – though she had an opinion. She LOVED you and told you so – even my husband can attest to this. I truly felt that I could tell my mom anything and that she would help me no matter what. She was my best friend, my business partner, my mentor. Her LOVE came through in her JOY for life.

Music is in most of my memories of my mom. When my mom was cleaning or redecorating (which was ALL the time), she would put on the music and sing. She would often break into song when you said something, like if I was shouting "STOP!" she'd sing, "In the name of love, before you break my heart." Or if I said, "Mom, I can't find my boots," she'd reply, "These boots are made for walking, and that's just what I'll do." It would be so infuriating, but she would be laughing and smiling, and eventually I would be laughing with her. Another fabulous memory was when Mom would set up her "stage." She would push the table back in her dining room to accommodate a dance party and who ever was in the room was pulled into dancing with her. If she wasn't singing along, she was clicking her tongue to the music. It hurts to re-live these memories, and there are so many more spilling from my heart. I love my mom for her silliness and her joy for life.

When my mom was diagnosed with pancreatic cancer in 2012, I cried until I was sobbing and couldn't breathe. I was so AFRAID. How could I go on without her? Who was going to be there for me? I could hear her saying, "It is all going to be okay," but I couldn't stop the fear from creeping in. How was it going to be okay without her? In the first few weeks after her diagnosis, my mom and I would go on early morning walks before I started work. We talked about anything and everything. I took her to Reiki treatments and we meditated together. I had the opportunity to thank her for her love and for her guidance in my life. I don't think my mom knew what people saw in her and how much she was loved by so many people in the community. She used to tell me all the time, "Today, I get to take another kick at the can," and she truly lived by that rule.

Man, I miss that lady and her strength and beauty.

I truly believe that my mom was ready to end her suffering. But I know she struggled when thinking of leaving us. Mom felt she kept us all together. She was our Strength, our ambassador for LOVE.

We were with Mom when her energy left her body. My sisters and I, my husband, my step-dad, Mom's sister, and her best friend. I saw her energy orb float outside her body and walk out of the room. It was so bright and beautiful it took my breath away. This beauty made me feel at peace for my mom. She was no longer suffering and I know that she loved me, and I know that she knew how much I loved her and was going to miss her. She told me before she died, "Tara you are my crier, but you have a strength within you and I can't wait to see what becomes of it." I am so thankful for her honesty with me.

I LOVE my life and I truly know that every moment in my life – good and bad – are part of this wonderful journey.

Now I get to embarrass my kids by singing to them! My son hates it when I wake him with the "Good morning" song. I love letting go and hearing my mom's voice in my heart saying, "Stop stressing, have fun!! Dance, Sing, LIVE!" I now have lip-sync jams in the car with the kids and dance parties in the kitchen. I am overjoyed to have four beautiful children. These tiny balls of energy are my greatest teachers of love; of JOY and strength. It is true what they say that having children is a feeling of your heart walking outside of your body. Our youngest daughter was born a year after my mom died. This little angel often reminds us to stop and "smell the roses." She is tenacious and has brought laughter back into our home. After being filled with such sadness and fear, I have been shown how to accept love again. Each one of our children has a different gift that I get to share, love, and guide. To see the world's beauty in the eyes of an innocent child is the great gift of LOVE.

It has been four years since my mom's diagnosis. I have grown immensely as a mother, as a wife, and as a woman. I have learned, as many of us do when we lose someone, that life is precious and that we need to cherish every moment. I still have many moments when the fear and loneliness start to make its way into my heart, but when I breathe and take a moment through meditation, I can see the energy around me and the Love that is waiting for me to embrace. Reiki allows me to still my mind and opens my heart to listen. Reiki has taught me to take some time each day to be one with love. We are energy and energy is Love. My journey is not over. I have much more love to give. I will take every moment of my past and use the teaching in my future.

By letting go of fear and anger, all that is left is LOVE - **Tara Nadia Campbell**

Tara Campbell is a working mother of four, a wife, a sister, a friend, and a healer. She is motivated to help others, and people are drawn to her warmth, insightful directness, compassion, and humor. As a former business owner and bra fitting specialist, Tara has spoken in small and large group settings on positive body image, work/life balance, and living with grief. Trained in Holy Fire Reiki Level 2, she has an increased self-awareness and a better understanding of how love can heal. This is Tara's first published work.

https://ca.linkedin.com/in/taranadiacampbell

Chapter 8

Reflection

by Tara Nadia Campbell

You are standing at an edge of a clearing. There is a beautiful lake in front of you and a long narrow dock in what looks like the very centre of the universe. The water is clear as glass and though there is a chill in the air, you can feel the warmth of the sun as it peeks through a break in the clouds. You walk towards the dock and notice that your feet are bare; you stretch out your toes to feel the grass and mud, and walk further towards the dock. As you walk out onto the dock, you stretch your arms out, palm up, opening yourself to the universe – asking for Love and healing. You can feel the cool energy from the stressful day leave through the balls of your feet and new warm energy expand from your hands through your entire body.

This is where my mind goes when I take a few moments to breathe: I reach the end of the dock in my mind and can see my reflection in the sky above me.

I share this with you because I wear a mask throughout my daily life. I smile, I listen, and I post positive things on Facebook. I go to work, drive my kids to their activities, clean the house, and get the groceries. I try to be engaged, but honestly, inside I am buzzing like a bee, trying to organize, plan, arrange, and sometimes just deal with the life I have created.

Now, let me tell you – I LOVE MY LIFE. I really honestly do, but it is busy and chaotic, and can be stressful. When I forget to take moments for myself, to breathe, it can easily become overwhelming.

In the past ten years, I cannot even begin to tell you how many times I have heard someone remark, "I don't know how you do it." I usually smile or laugh and say, "Some days I don't know either." But the truest answer is that I don't know any other way. This is the life that I have and this is the way I live it.

When I was growing up, I was raised by a very strong, confident, and spiritual woman. I felt safe with her, and loved, and she gave me the gift of her confidence in the joy that life brings us.

I know that this is the life I was meant to live. Sometimes we get taken off course a little as our ego, or fear, gets in the way. I often get on the phone when it gets overwhelming and talk out what is rambling in my mind, and then after I have spewed out the noise that is in my head, I begin to listen. This is when I take myself to the end of the dock. It helps me to move forward and remember the LOVE that I have for my life.

I encourage you to take a few moments in your life to breathe. It is in these moments of standing still that we can truly see the love that is all around us.

Dream BIG, Love with your whole heart, and trust in yourself.

Tara Campbell is a working mother of four, a wife, a sister, a friend, and a healer. She is motivated to help others, and people are drawn to her warmth, insightful directness, compassion, and humor. As a former business owner and bra fitting specialist, Tara has spoken in small and large group settings on positive body image, work/life balance, and living with grief. Trained in Holy Fire Reiki Level 2, she has an increased self-awareness and a better understanding of how love can heal. This is Tara's first published work.

https://ca.linkedin.com/in/taranadiacampbell

Chapter 9

Love and Gratitude for the Future

by Joey Wargachuk

Every Morning I wake up and take in my first deep breath, open my eyes wide, and I speak the words "Thank You." The gratitude I am feeling inside me vibrates and grows from deep inside my heart beating in my chest and moves up and outward, filling the bedroom of my apartment, growing at the speed of light, cosmically washing over the city of Toronto I call home and out into the universe.

I feel so truly blessed to be alive and live in this extraordinary time of the 21st century. I love all of the modern conveniences we have that make my life so easy: running water, alternating current, and the cell phone I love so much! I not only say thank you to all the inventors and creators, I also give thanks for the countless and nameless plumbers who connected and advanced modern plumbing. I resonate with Nikola Tesla's love of electricity bestowing us with thousands of ways to use and harnesses energy – such as creating a smart phone that connects billions of people instantly. Could you even imagine life with out your smart phone? Ha! I give thanks every millisecond for plugs surging with juice for my lights and gadgets. I don't ever think of what life would be like with out any of it! I resonate on the love of those things greeting them with thanks!

It's such a beautiful and exciting time to be alive! City landscapes twinkle and grow like steel weeds shining in the sky that is swarming with satellites beaming back photos of this wonderful blue and green world that fill me with awe and wonder! I get so excited when I see an online article on

Facebook or a blog about an amazing new invention or discovery that is being made and created almost every minute on this remarkable planet. Please take it all in. Feel with me the joy and gratitude of everything we have as a human race. We are living in ways that, even one hundred years ago, no one could have dreamed of in the wildest of science fiction.

We Are Living in the Future! We are Loving in the Future! We are the children of the dreams and love of those before us. This future is our inheritance, as I reflect on that. I feel immense love that fills every atom of my being radiating gratitude that the words "Thank You" are joyfully pure. Love is the force that hurtles us to our future and brings change and progress for a better, brighter day for children and their children. Love is what brought us the renaissance and out of the dark ages. Love and passion is unlocking all the secrets of the universe and sharing it for the good and love of all. I love the future, for it is a new day. May each new day for you be filled with love and light, always and forever.

Joey Wargachuk is an entrepreneur, Tarot & Crystal Reader, digital marketing guru, and a certified Usui Reiki master/teacher (Levels I, II, and Master). From a young age, intuition spiritual practices have been a dramatic part of his life. Joey now derives great joy from healing those around him by helping them find their better path through Reiki, Tarot & Crystal readings.

Chapter 10

Follow the Messages and Signs
by Karen Phelps

Growing up, I personally felt a little different and distant from others around me. However, if you knew me then, you would probably disagree and see me as the spoiled "Golden Child." Being the first-born girl in the family for a couple of generations led to lots of love. I was born with red hair and freckles (which during school caused me torment).

My grandparents were heavily involved with our upbringing (due to our parents being very young – still kids themselves, actually). This allowed our parents to go work full-time and begin building a future for us. I spent a great deal of time at my grandparents' cottage and always sensed somebody was in the room with me, watching me, but I never saw them.

We grew up in a very small village in Worcestershire in the UK. It was a lovely and safe place to play as a kid. All the families socialized together well, which meant my brother and I were exposed to hanging out with kids of all ages – older and younger than ourselves. This built a great foundation to our personalities today.

We quickly learned respect and appreciation for everyone. We made mistakes like every other family, but we learned from them mainly because our grandparents demanded it.

Looking back, I realize they were all lessons to teach me to build the life I have now.

Fast forward thirty years.

I now live in Ontario, Canada. I am married to an amazing, supportive, funny, and well-educated guy. We have no kids but we have a dog. It's a puppy we rescued from being euthanized, whom we love very much and who teaches us things about love and communication every day.

I no longer work for anyone else. I am lucky enough to be able to stay at home and do the things that are important to me.

Throughout my life experiences, I still had a feeling of being a bit different to others. I've always had lots of friends from many different walks of life and most of them have always had the same message for me: *I have a great way of supporting and respecting them. I am a friend they know that no matter what, they can rely on me to be there for them.*

I'm not a very good person when it comes to accepting compliments or believing in myself, but the message has always been consistent. So I began to listen.

Even when I have been brutally honest with my opinions when asked, most of the time they have always continued to be close to me.

I feel everyone sees me as this confident person that can achieve anything but isn't that all of us?

The reality is I'm actually not a very confident person at all, but when I feel passionate about something and learn to love it, then my confidence grows.

I'm now in my 40s heading closer to my 50s. When you reach this age in life, you realize that you're old enough to look back and learn from your past, but young enough to put right what needs to change for your future, should you feel you need to.

The past eight years have been the most challenging, exciting, emotional, and happiest times so far of my life.

Why?

Many reasons, probably very similar to others reading this.

The main rationales are: loss of loved ones, family issues and challenges, illnesses, work, and marriage. That's life, right?

Some people are just dealt really bad luck and have had to live through a lot worse than my experiences.

My Mom has always said, "There'll always be someone worse off than yourself. Remember that."

They were her last words to me on her death bed.

It's how you deal with it that determines the recovery and for some people there is none.

My heart goes out to those ones.

My mom died at the age of sixty-three to a lung disease. Mom was in hospital with my dad at her side.

Mom had been really strong struggling with this disease for almost three years, but she was tired and wanted to be with her mom. We had discussed many times before about life after death and how we both believed in Angels, spirits, and life after death. This helped when the time came, but nothing can really prepare you to say goodbye. Mom was extremely frightened to let go and really upset that she wouldn't see her grandkids grow up. Mom passed away like a hero though. She remained strong and organized till the end. I was with her. She had waited for me to be there.

I knew it was time and helped her let go of her life here because I knew I had to. I could sense my grandmother (her mom) waiting at the other end. That night, my mom's mom had answered my prayers because as I drove to the hospital that night, I begged my "Nanny" to take her daughter back and she did.

It was pure love, but heartache watching my dad, who was also there, not wanting her to leave him but knew he had no choice.

I truly learned the meaning of the circle of life that day. I understood immediately that there are just some things in life we have no control over and we have to accept that. Otherwise it will take over your own life. It's what happens in between that is important.

I believe things happen for a reason. I had to sit back, take a look at my life, and see what before I had either chosen to ignore or it was pure blind to me.

There are many signs and messages out there for us. You have to look and listen for them.

Those loved ones that I have lost recently, and that's not just my mom, have confirmed to me that if you allow them to communicate with you, they will. I get messages all the time. Sometimes it can be a voice in my head or a feeling in my stomach. Other times, it can be something I see.

Still there are times that I am uncertain if it is a message or not, but I turn my frequency up a notch and stay on amber alert. If I get the same feeling again soon after, I know its a message to go with it. This is now where I feel much more confident with myself and more determined to follow my dreams because life is shortly lived.

I'm trying to teach others around me the same. Listen to your body and what is it telling you. If something doesn't feel right, stop ignoring it.

To help me deal with my own emotions and to help others, because helping others has always been my number one aim, I decided to take the Reiki 1 and Reiki 2 courses. I was tired and exhausted, and had enough of really hard changes and challenges.

I needed to get away and have some alone time. My husband was really supportive and wished me well. "Go do what you gotta do," he said.

I drove to a Yoga retreat and spent time in my own thoughts. I took the 2 Reiki courses back to back and met some amazing women there wanting to practice Reiki for similar reasons. It was perfect.

We spent time practicing Reiki on one another and sharing our experiences through this whole process. Reiki is just the most amazing natural therapy to me.

My senses to this healing work through my hands, my heart, and my head not only comfort me, but comfort my clients too. I began my own business treating others with Reiki and Thai foot massage reflexology almost two years ago, working from home.

I trust things more, mainly my inner voice and instinct. I am amazed how my hands can tell me things about a person I am treating and it feels so good to help them.

I am a more patient person now. I trust things more because the signs and messages sent to me have never disappointed me. They may not always be what I want to know but they are normally warning me to be aware of something or to embrace it.

When I have a new client or feel something is not right, I call upon my friend who is a Reiki Master to guide me. I have learned to ask for help, which is a sign of strength, not a sign of weakness. I know that now.

My days are more relaxed and calmer because I trust myself and the Reiki. I listen to the messages in my head and the pictures that I see as I walk my life.

This is my journey now: *True Freedom.*

My life has been enlightened through experiences and lessons learned. I understand there are some things you have no control over and other things that can be influenced by change if you're willing to put the effort in. Reiki helps me accept them either way.

Acceptance is everything to me. I am truly blessed.

Karen Phelps became a Reiki Practitioner because she realized that the Mind, Body, & Soul talk to us and send messages. We just have to take the time to listen to them, and to live a happier, healthier, more balanced life style. For many people, they believe they are "too busy" or are not willing to try because they're afraid what it will mean or what they have to do. Karen also began practicing Thai Foot Massage Reflexology and likes to combine the two treatments together. She continues to study her Holistic approach to life and provides many natural benefits to her clients.

gingeincanada@hotmail.ca

Chapter 11

Wings of Love
by Trina Virgin

The Church pews are full of people, waiting with quiet expectation. I am standing at the podium holding a little green, iridescent, stuffed dragon. All eyes are on me, and all I want to do is cry. I feel the grief ooze out of this beloved treasure. I hear a child giggling near my left ear. A sudden chill washes over me and the words begin to flow quickly. Mom and Grandmother weep, as I describe the little boy that brought such joy and left too soon. He is no longer in pain. I assure them he is held in the arms of his great grandmother on the other side, and to remember that love is eternal.

I am a Medium; someone who has learned how to communicate with pets and people after they have made their transition to heaven, or through the veil as some would call it. Our hearts break because of the absence of physical touch and not ever being able to hear their voice again. Sadness overwhelms us with the realization that there is no longer anything tangible to hold onto, except memories. I am the messenger who helps bring closure and heals the emptiness that threatens to consume us, while going through the bereavement process. It is by no means the only way through recovery. I encourage everyone to explore different therapies and tools to find what works best for them so that they can move on and find peace. Most people are thrown out of their comfort zone and all that was familiar in their lives, especially when an unexpected death has occurred. We must find ways to face the challenges in learning how to live without those who will always be dear to us.

Not everyone gets to a chance to say goodbye or repair a tattered relationship, be it a friend or family member. The spirit's personality comes through clearly. If someone was a miserable person here, that is how they the present themselves to me, so you can recognize them. They don't become angelic overnight, although their outlook may have softened because they see things from a different perspective. Depending how long they have been in spirit, they understand better what could have been and may ask for forgiveness. They might tell you to let go of guilt you may be still carrying because you were not able to be present when they took their last breath. I am privileged to be a witness and a facilitator in mending the bonds of love.

Unfortunately, I know from firsthand experience exactly how a loss feels. I never imagined a tragedy ever touching my family of this magnitude. My life plan certainly has taken many detours. I would have preferred the merry-go-round version of a simple uneventful life. I must have said before incarnating, "Give me a bit of everything. I can handle it!" That is what I got, although the scary roller coaster version of life is for own growth. No one in their right mind would deliberately choose hardship to achieve Nirvana. I guess that's why when we come through the birth canal, we forget what we agreed to do. Or maybe that's why birth is so painful. The baby does remember and has changed its mind. Something to think about!

It is an amazing feat that I can stand in front of a crowd at all. I was an incredibly sensitive, shy child and preferred my imaginary friends and talking to animals. That was until my teen years when boys became more interesting than chasing the elusive forest fairy. In my 20's, my mother-in-law gave me a deck of tarot cards, took me to yoga and meditation classes, and that reawakened my fascination with the unseen.

September 10th, 2001: my world changed dramatically. Our nineteen-year-old son passed away. It took me a long time to come to terms with his death. My heart shattered as did everyone else who knew and loved him. Everyone grieves differently in the face of loss and depends on the relationship you had with that person. My father passed a few years before, and the grief process was so different than that of my child who I carried for nine months and had such aspirations for. I was angry with God. I decided I wanted nothing more to do with anything spiritual again. I questioned why we are here and why we have to endure so much pain.

Soon after Matthew died, I began having dreams of him. I could smell his cologne around the house. From time to time I could see flashes of light out of the corner of my eye while sitting in my living room. I wondered if in my grief, my grip on reality was seriously slipping farther and farther into the black hole I was on the edge of, because I had a very precarious hold already.

A couple, whose son had passed the year before, came to visit. Their belief had been that after death, the body was just an empty shell, having no soul or essence to incarnate. Many people hold similar ideas and that's why I am cautious about saying what I do, even though their deceased loved one may be standing behind them with a wide grin. In that situation, I don't say a word as it kind of freaks people out. I'm just not comfortable with being branded as weird or called a witch for some reason. That has happened. This particular couple's anguish led them to see a local woman who called herself a Medium. I had never heard the term before, or that someone other than a highly evolved being like Jesus or a mystic like Teresa of Avila could communicate with Angels or even the Almighty. Their view on death changed with the reading and they were inspired to share their story. I made an appointment and did some research on what exactly a Medium did before I sat with her. This caring woman's description and accuracy of my son helped mend my fragile heart. I knew this was something I wanted to learn to do. It was not until about a year later, I began to go to classes with a local teacher and at the spiritualist church an hour away. I was hungry to learn and it has been a long process birthing my gifts and trusting the information I receive through my senses.

Along the way my heart began to heal as well as my relation to infinite spirit. That childhood sensitivity is called empathy. As a spirit draws close during a reading, I feel within my body the aches and pains that resided in their body and I get a sense of how they passed. I am overwhelmed with the abundance of love that comes through for the sitter. My wild imagination helps me to describe exactly what someone's mom's quirky humor and vibrant character was like. I can smell the delicious fresh baked bread someone loved to eat. It's awesome when it's something delicious; not so much when its stinky feet!

Those in spirit try very hard to let you know they are near. It may be a significant song coming on the radio that triggers a memory or a butterfly that lands on your shoulder. It used to be pennies falling from heaven – now its nickels and dimes or feathers in unusual places. It's your relatives and friends for sure. Sometimes we dismiss it, but they are very creative in their attempts to get you to pay attention. Please believe me when I tell you – it is real!

We all have free will with how we choose to face the challenges that come our way. Instead of closing down, I blossomed and have embraced my spiritual gifts. I am grateful for the many inspiring people I have met along this crazy path that I was brave enough to travel on. I had to learn about self-love and to be fully present with my pain before I could be of help to another. While I am here, I make the most of each day and my bucket list is still not finished. I am linked to both worlds. My son and dad are part of my team of angels and guides. "My peeps" is the way I fondly refer to them as. I call on my team when I am giving messages. As the Joni Mitchel song says, *"I've looked at love from both sides now,"* and I have.

I feel my Matthew's presence as I write this on the anniversary of his death. Even after all these years, those special occasions such as a birthday and Christmas still make my heart ache for him. Around those times, I slip into my funk as I like to call it and I ride that wave until it passes.

My oldest son still gets together with Matthew's friends to raise a glass or two as a way of remembering him by on the anniversary of his crossing, always in the same place where they used to play as kids. Matthew left an impression on everyone he met as evidenced by those who want to come out each year.

We all have our rituals to remember those who have passed and those rituals may change and evolve over time. I believe we are here to grow, evolve, and do whatever brings joy. Like weeds breaking through cracks in the pavement, I believe we come equipped with a strong will to flourish despite the obstacles put in our way.

Remember the famous Wayne Dyer quote: *"Don't die with your music still in you."*

My wish is for everyone to grow more beautiful inside and out and more loving despite the messiness of life.

The phrase "I love you" has so much more meaning because they could be the last words you ever hear. I make sure I say it to family members and close friends. I make sure I tell someone how much their conversation and time together means to me. My heart was like a wilted black rose and now I feel like an ever-growing garden in full array of color. I am a messenger. The words flow down from heaven on the wings of love and it's been an amazing journey.

Blessings

Trina Virgin

Trina Virgin is a mother of two and proud grandmother of three, who currently lives in the Guelph area. Since she has developed a case of wanderlust, who knows where she will be in five years. Trina has been on a spiritual journey for many years and learned to connect with loved ones, guides, and the angelic realm. Writing has also become a passion. Trina offers Mediumship and Angel guidance readings.

trinavirgin@hotmail.com

Facebook "Wings of Love"

Chapter 12

The Journey of Love
by Candace Hawkshaw

On my journey in this life, I have had it all, lost it all, and now I only wish to be healthy, happy, and share my life with those who resonate with me. I was in the world of competition; sex was love. I had to have the big house, the car, the high paying job, work, and be at the top. Now I wish to be love, serve love, and share my love with the world. Yes of course I require a home, food, a car, and money. That is a given because that is how we live in this world.

I became a Reiki Master back in the late 90's. I found it very hard to request money for my Reiki healing. I asked the question, "How do I put a price on Love?" I have always felt and still do feel that Reiki is love, the highest energy in the Universe. Can we not pay a person with love?

In this world, money has been considered corrupt, dark – all those programmed words we were told – money doesn't grow on trees; you have to work hard for your money. What if each time we received money, we blessed it and cleared that energy? What if we serve through love and people could pay us what they could, so they could heal and be loved?

I recently started offering some of my classes at a lower price. I feel everyone should learn Reiki because it is the most beautiful love in the world. Placing your healing hands on yourself and sending healing is a wonderful way to start and end your day. Once you have felt this or experienced this love, trust me, you will never be the same again. Once you learn about energy and how it can affect those around you, you will be more aware of your thoughts, your actions, and what choices you are making in your life. Reiki helps you look deep within yourself and guides you to love – it is love.

I have witnessed people come closer to their love and their family through Reiki. When I do sessions for couples, I see that they reconnect and remember all the love they have for each other. Love Heals.

What I learn I teach others: language, choice, actions, Reiki, and assist them to find who they are, not what others say they are or all the identities that are bestowed upon them.

I know when I worked in the corporate world it could get pretty nasty sometimes, with the competition and the gossip. If I knew back then what I know now, I would have been in a better place in my whole being.

It is really about loving ourselves, having boundaries, choices, speaking, standing in our truth, and always being in integrity. If we do not have boundaries, people will walk all over us and we will create resentment for others. Standing in our truth can be tough because we have all these fears that come up, such as: Will they not like me? What will they think? Will I lose my job? If we make choices in our lives in fear and we are not standing in who we are, that can leave many blocks within our being, staying there hanging around us, sometimes eating away at us. Questions arise like: Why didn't I say no? Why did I do that? Why don't I like going there or doing that? Did I do that out of guilt or obligation? You would feel so much lighter and freer if you stood your ground and said "No" in the first place, because it did not feel right in the core of your being.

I read Akashic records, so I have seen the blocks that are holding people back in this life from past choices. The records are registered the moment you are created as a Soul. Each choice or action you take is recorded in these records which get carried with you for many lifetimes until you clear these blocks. One example: we are here to experience and be love as Divine Beings, correct? So, can you imagine how a person feels when they go to war and actually witness and are a part of the death of others? That literally eats them up inside and their essence as a Divine being. When I look at their web that surrounds them, it is either torn or trying to heal. The web connects a person to the weave which connects us all together. Sometimes it gets so bad, they remove themselves from the Divine weave totally. They may feel empty, sad, or depressed because they are connecting directly to the Divine Life Force Energies. I love this part of how I help people see and understand the choices they made or make and how they affect us for a long time, possibly lifetimes.

We all have free wills, but we can give them away if we do not stop and say no, speak truth, and stand in our own integrity.

I have learned that I am on my own journey and I will stand in my integrity and authenticity. I am not responsible for what others are doing. When I see something in someone that bothers me, I look deep into myself to see what they are mirroring in me. I am still learning and healing parts of myself. I no longer think about what people are saying about me. I know who I am. Reiki was a huge part of my growth and healing. It has assisted me staying in alignment with who I am, balance, being peace, and filled with love. I believe that the Universe always has our back and we are where we are meant to be in that moment in our lives.

My passion is to love, be loved, and help others get there: to love, be loved and Love.

Blessings.

In Love, Candace

Candace Hawkshaw is a certified Holy Fire II Reiki Master, a teacher, a healer, and a mentor. She is certified in many other complementary healing modalities, and is the bridge that will connect your Soul and Spirit to the Universal Source. Candace is a weaver of Love, who will assist you on your journey to remember who you are and your purpose!! Her business is called Know Thyself. She is an international teacher. Candace has written her stories in three books: The Ruby Red Shoes – Empowering Stories on Relationships, Intuition & Purpose, Living Without Limitations – Vision Quest, & #Peace – A New Perspective of Hope.

http://www.know-thyself.ca

https://www.facebook.com/candacenhawkshaw/

Chapter 13

Love Your Scars
by Danielle Hughes

Unconditional self love is a daily choice. It comes through when you can truly let go of the Ego that whispers quietly of all your "failures" or "weaknesses." The Ego is fed by bullies and toxic people in your life who point out all of these things and cause you to question yourself. Have you ever said no to something you wanted to do? Have you denied your truth when speaking to others? Have you ever had a negative thought related to self-image float into your mind unbidden? These are examples of the whispers that can undermine your true self-love. Unconditional self-love comes from your Highest Self and transcends all; there are no qualifications or limitations. It is through the healing of our inner wounds and embracing the Shadow Self that we can truly attain this.

Life is a series of experiences, choices, and interactions. Many interactions become beautiful memories, however some leave behind a different kind of memento. There are some interactions that can cause bumps, bruises, and wounds to our emotional and mental selves. Wounds tend to develop scars that can be difficult to deal with – a scar does not simply disappear on its own. Being aware of those scars is the first step; falling back into unconditional love with yourself is the second. The journey to healing occurs in stages and levels. As you move deeper into the healing, a spark of self-love ignites and grows brighter and brighter. When you make a decision to achieve whole self-healing, it must be done through love to succeed. Love creates a bridge for healing to flow through your entire being with comfort and support. The final stage of healing calls you to release and let go of all the walls and coverings that you use to hide your scars from the world. When you can shed these trappings, and stand tall and proud at the final gate, all that is gloriously you, true unconditional love can come in.

It is through unconditional self-love that you can find all the old wounds, and through love, forgiveness, and time, heal them. The love of self is a powerful vibration that reverberates through your entire life. There is nothing selfish in becoming unconditionally loving with yourself. You'll find that you have more to give to others.

When we can look deep within and not only be aware of the scars of old wounds, but proudly bear those scars, a truly complete healing occurs. Love always finds a way. Through love comes the most profound healing – that which pours through you mind, body, and spirit. Stand proud and love your scars.

Danielle Hughes received her Reiki I attunement at sixteen years of age and has studied under many teachers to create her unique approach to healing mind, body, and spirit. Danielle works through a heart-centered approach to provide unique sessions for each person. She has written in several anthologies and writes for a monthly publication.

www.facebook.com/EarthWisdoms

Chapter 14

Loving Light Energy of Holy Fire and the Angels
by Suzanne Bertolas

My name is Suzanne Bertolas and I am a Usui / Holy Fire II / Angel Fire Reiki Master and teacher who works directly with the Angelic Realm. Because of this, my life has changed in so many incredible ways – at times it is simply breathtaking.

The most noticeable transformation in my life is that I am now very aware of the waves of unconditional love that we are showered with on a daily basis from our creator.

I see this in a major way during my Reiki sessions with clients when they experience the love from the Holy Fire Energy. It is wonderful to see a client relax and let their burdens dissipate as they trust in the process of healing with the loving light energy of God and the Angels.

For more than three decades, I have worked in the cosmetology industry, helping women with their hair and self-empowerment. Being a stylist is like being a councillor. We are trusted with the deepest secrets and heartfelt life issues of our clients and quite often we are used as a sounding board.

It was during the years while working closely with clients, I realized I had a deep sense of knowing and a gift of hearing higher messages from the Angels that my clients were meant to receive.

I became comfortable very quickly in passing these messages along. Each time the messages I would give were received with enthusiasm and understanding, I was encouraged to continue to develop my skill. This gift of intuition would come into play in a big way once I started on my path with Reiki.

I learned at a young age how important it is to embrace compassion and empathy, to be friendly and giving when another soul places their heart in your hands. It is extremely humbling to be allowed into the energetic field of someone who may be in desperate need of regaining self-worth and love for themselves.

This is something I do not take lightly and I hold the utmost respect for the friends I have gained who have trusted me with their hearts during a healing session.

Reiki and helping others heal is a way of life for me, but of course I go through growth spurts of releasing negative blocks and gaining truth and understanding about myself, like everyone else. However, Holy Fire Reiki constantly flows through me to help me on my journey of loving and understanding myself and the world around me.

Once we have a firm grasp on understanding how hard personal growth can be, it allows us to show the greatest amount of humility towards another person who may by struggling with their own life.

If we understand this, we understand love.

Suzanne Bertrolas is an Angel Fire Reiki Master/Teacher, and an Angel Intuitive Healer. She is the author of her own book and the designer of her own Angel Encouragement cards, which she uses for private readings and on her YouTube channel for general readings.

scouchman@rogers.com

Chapter 15

Love Empathy
by Natalie Friese

May my soul bloom in love for all existence - Rudolf Steiner

I was born an empath. Perhaps being a twin instantly birthright's you empathic abilities? I remember being in a separate incubator from my identical sister and touching the glass trying to get to her, to calm her pain. I also remember being bottle fed by my exhausted father and feeling his every emotion. Growing up, I was not a stranger to emotional and physical connection. Someone would say, "My stomach hurts," and I'd reply, "Yeah, it does! Are you okay?" I don't think they actually knew that I could literally feel their every symptom.

I also knew from a very young age that I didn't like to inflict pain on to others for the very obvious reason of that awful feedback loop – empathy. As a way to survive and live in peace, I quickly learned to create boundaries.

Too often I hear "The world needs more empathy." Though I feel that empathy is a beautiful tool, I'd like to clarify that empathy itself is not an act of love. This ability, if not understood well and then grounded in love, could cause you to stray away from experiencing true and unconditionally loving relationships.

Compassion, however, requires love. Compassion demands putting all emotions (yours and others') aside to lead with love. The world indeed needs more compassion.

Empathy is the ability to feel deeply – beyond your internal self and into the external world. Though the action of empathy can be done out of love, the act itself is not necessarily loving.

Empathy is a sensible way to feel or embody someone else's feelings (physical and emotional).

To be empathic means that you can literally tune into someone else's "channel" and sense their experience – though, thankfully, only partially. This doesn't mean we should avoid tuning into empathy. Life has gifted us with a self-defence mechanism so that we will never be completely burdened with someone else's pain in addition to our own.

Empathy is never purely unbiased. As expressed by Anais Nin, *"We don't see things as they are, we see them as we are."*

Empathy helps protect us by giving us the ability to gage our environment. The more empathic you are, the more you can sense the intensity of a situation.

Having too much empathy, however (or not knowing how to deal with the feelings created by it), can lead to self-sacrifice; the destruction of oneself for another. This act is often confused with compassion and the act of service. You feel so "bad" for someone that you want to take away their pain often at a cost to your own life.

What many do not realize is that taking away someone else's pain often means taking control of the other individual's freedom of choice. Our overzealous empathic feelings steer us away from being able to perform acts of love with compassion.

In Buddhism, compassion and love are seen as one and the same. Compassion represents the desire for someone's eternal freedom, and love, as desiring someone's eternal happiness.

A truly compassionate act will come from a place of love and freedom from all individuals involved.

It's easy to say that we want someone to be happy. The challenge is to accept that their happiness can only be achieved through their own free will.

Interestingly, if we want to experience true love for ourselves (i.e. to be free and happy), we have to practice compassion for ourselves to accept our innermost desires and free ourselves from our attachments. This, in turn, releases and inspires others to follow their true desire function.

Rudolf Steiner quotes *"Freedom is the sense of being capable of actions motivated solely by love."*

We often get stuck in attachment because of our own sense of empathy. We feel deeply for the other individual and so we get stuck in the very feedback loop of emotion that I mentioned earlier. We become attached to "feeling bad" for them instead of "feeling love" for them, while trusting that they can take care of themselves.

Victimizing yourself and dimming your own light for someone else certainly doesn't light the way. If you want to light-up a clear path for yourself and for humanity, then shine brighter by loving deeper. Establish boundaries for times when you may not have enough light to share and trust that others can find the resources they need to light their own way.

Compassion is a beautiful moral ability, often provoked in the purest of hearts. It is about seeing suffering in a kind and loving way. It is not about making suffering disappear. It's the hug, the breath, and the stillness. It is the purity of love and comes solely from a place of love, not from a place of worry, fear, or guilt. You can feel the pain through empathy but you let it go with compassion

It has been suggested that compassion is a form of intelligence. To be truly compassionate, you have to use your head and your heart. You have to find complete resonance within your intellect and your will. If you only think about love, you won't feel it, and it is impossible to consciously feel love without acknowledging it.

Try picturing the famous Tibetan monk when he speaks of the hurt and chaos in the world. Does he not continue to smile and radiate loving energy? His forehead doesn't frown, his tone isn't angered, and his posture isn't repressed. He speaks from peace because he has tapped into his inner unconditional love. He knows that the greatest change will occur as a result of his continuous spreading of love. He remains calm, serene, and compassionate.

As a Doctor of Medical Heilkunst (a system for Whole Healing), Spiritual Guide, and Empath, I accept my clients for who they are and what they want to do. Where they want to go and how they want to feel is truly up to them. I listen and I care. I tap in with empathy but I love with compassion.

I am not here to change you. I am here to love – to love you, myself, the world, and life.

Your truth is only known in the resonance of your being. Love evolves – it doesn't involve. Love is being, and accepting others being.

If you can learn to use empathy to participate in the world while grounding it in compassion, you will never fall out of tune.

May YOUR soul bloom in love for all existence.

Namaste,

Natalie Friese

Natalie Friese and her family own a successful Health Store, Holistic Health Clinic, Education Center, and Green Smoothie Bar in Cambridge, Ontario. She is a Canadian natural health industry expert, professional supplement formulator, published writer, inspirational speaker, and health educator. Her teachings aim to empower people to root themselves in their inherent wisdom, so that they live a life that is more whole and enriched with the things that really matter. On a personal note, Natalie has a love for world travel, celebrating the sacred feminine, holistic nutrition and cooking, swimming, essential oils, and enjoying time with her family and friends.

www.naturesvibe.ca

Chapter 16

Musings of a Romantic Heart
by Danielle Hughes

When we talk about love, most people think of romantic love first. Love comes in many forms: family, friends, pets, and of course spouses. I grew up as a voracious reader and I loved all the tales of a romantic nature. As a teen, I was more interested in fantasizing about romantic heroes or the *Phantom of the Opera* than the latest boyband. Not that I didn't experience the usual crushes that are a rite of passage as a teenager, but they were not as intense nor was I as engaged with them as my peers at the time. And so, I was what many may consider a late bloomer when I came to the dating game. I had no interest in passing fancy – I wanted something more. I wanted something I could not yet define.

I am not sure I could define it still to this day. I have learned so much about relationships and the different forms of spiritual relationships there are. Each one has its joys and its hardships, but they all provide lessons and teach us how to love ourselves deeper. I truly believe that as we set out into each lifetime we also determine which types of relationships will help to expand our spiritual growth and bring us closer to wholeness. Each lifetime is an opportunity to learn, to grow, and to expand ourselves.

When we come into a lifetime, we could experience Karmic Relationships, Soul Mate Relationships, or A Twin Flame Relationship if we choose. Some lifetimes we may choose to forgo long-term romantic relationships as it will not provide the lessons needed to evolve, and other lifetimes may be filled with karmic and soul mate connection potentials. It all comes down to what is your soul's direction and what will help you to achieve the learning needed to evolve to the next level. At the end of the day, we are all love and we all come from love. It's just a matter of deciding on how we are going to express it this time around.

Depending on where we are in our soul's journey, the first type of relationship we become involved in are **Karmic Relationships**. Sometimes we live a lifetime of karmic relationships as we work through our ability to find self-love, self-worth, and the ability to engage in the outer world without fear of the expectations of society, our families, and our inner shadows, which all play a role in the karmic relationship.

Karmic relationships burn fast and bright, then fizzle out to nothingness. It is in that nothingness we must be careful not to become attached or addicted to this form of relationship. It is easy to get caught in a cycle of control, jealousy, or victimization that can occur. Karmic relationships are sometimes the hardest because they are never meant to last. They may feel exciting and intense, but that fades quickly and then we are left to deal with the shadow of it. It is easy to get caught up in the memory of the excitement and not want to let it go. But let it go we must. These relationships quickly turn into manipulative and sometimes abusive situations. The longer we remain in the karmic relationship, the harder it is to walk away and the longer the healing process afterwards. Be cautious in these relationships because they can trigger your own tendencies towards manipulation, jealousy, and anger.

Our karmic romances can be easily identified by their ability to bring out the absolute worst in ourselves – they are meant to teach us how to deal with the shadows, and balance them with light. Karmic lovers are often selfish and more concerned with themselves and how you can help them, with no real thought to what it is you need. Many times, they bring forward the martyr in us, which adds to the addiction of the relationship. We see the karmic lover as someone we need to save, when what we really need to do is save ourselves.

Karmic relationships teach us how to heal ourselves and as we heal, we realize how much our vibration attracts the type of people who surround us.

Soulmate Relationships tend to come in after the completion of our karmic lesson with karmic relationships. There are many forms of soulmate relationships: friends, lovers, mentors, family members. A soulmate is a person whose soul is from the same soul family as your own. Soulmates often are people we have experienced many lifetimes and lessons with, and there is an instant connection when we meet. Soulmate relationships have their own form of intensity, but it is rooted in a deep and stable love for each other.

When we meet a soulmate, there is an instant recognition and sense of comfort. The beauty in these relationships is that they can be as simple as a dandelion and as complex as a rose at the same time. Soulmates encourage our ability to self-evolve through challenging our inner-most beliefs of ourselves and how we reflect these values in our dealings with the world. Because a soulmate comes from a place of true and selfless love, they provide the support we need to delve deeper into our innermost selves, and to being the process of piecing together who we truly are.

Soulmate romantic relationships often feel safe, comforting, and despite their challenges, primarily flow in ease and grace. Some soulmates are meant to stay with us for the long term while other soulmate relationships are temporary. When a romantic soulmate relationship comes to an end, it is often a friendly and mutual parting of ways that allows for continued mutual respect and care.

The fabled Twin Flame Relationship is one that is still being understood. Twin flames used to be extremely rare but as we continue to raise our consciousness as a planet, twin flame relationships become more common.

The twin flame is an interesting relationship and often the hardest; therefore they mainly occur in the last few lifetimes of reincarnation. Twin flames are believed to be a single soul that has been split into two and incarnated in different bodies. Our twin flame is truly a mirror image of ourselves; this means having all our best and worst qualities reflected constantly.

Twin flame relationships are intense but unlike karmic relationships, they do not have the flash burn effect. Twin flames have a different form of intensity that comes from the deep inner knowledge that they are working through the final threads of Ego-centered lessons. Twin flames are not meant to be your "other half," they are meant to help you to develop and evolve into your whole self through their challenges and lessons. They have some of the same comforts as the soulmate relationship in the sense of a deep inner connection, but because twin flames are mirrors, they are complete opposites.

The opposition of the twin flame creates a delicate balance between challenging us and complementing us. This paired with the ability to feel comfortable with them as we would a soulmate creates the perfect storm for the final coming together of the lesson of Earth and human incarnation.

Twin flames come together in the understanding that this will be a long and difficult process to complete the karmic lessons within themselves while trying to develop the comfort and harmony seen in many soulmate relationships. However, even once harmony is attained, twin flames find a deeper layer to challenge us at. The twin flame relationship will always be intense and riddled with highs and lows, but it can take us down a deep and winding path that leads to complete inner wholeness.

The twin flame phenomenon is one that is still being explored. There is much that we do not understand about this type of romantic relationship. It is an interesting one because it has similarities to both karmic relationships and soulmate relationships.

Each form of romantic relationship provides value and learning. There are times I yearn for the quick fire of the initial stages of the karmic relationship despite knowing that it will not last. Some days, I dream of a comfortable and harmonious soulmate relationship where I have the cocoon of safety and support to delve deep within my inner self. Twin flame relationships seem to be the most bittersweet, because once they come into our lives, we know that our time is almost up and that the lessons of this world are almost at an end. Do I know truly what I am looking for in the next romantic encounter? No, but I understand that it will bring the lessons I need to come closer to my ability for greater self-love, a greater loving connection with the Universe, and all within in.

Danielle Hughes received her Reiki I attunement at sixteen years of age and has studied under many teachers to create her unique approach to healing mind, body, and spirit. Danielle works through a heart-centered approach to provide unique sessions for each person. She has written in several anthologies and writes for a monthly publication.

www.facebook.com/EarthWisdoms

Chapter 17

The Reluctant Messenger
by Trina Virgin

So, what do you do? It's a question often asked. My response is usually, "I work with kids." While the answer is true, it also does not reflect me entirely. For years I felt like I have led a secret life. For a long time, I saw myself as the reluctant messenger. I have struggled with low self-esteem and used to be extremely shy. I believe we all have a soul plan. We do have free will and can choose the way we want to live: struggling or surrendering and going with the flow. Many times, during my darkest, painful moments, I would have given anything to have a life filled with only joy. But the duality of love and loss is what we are here to experience. One of my lessons is to find my voice and not hide who I am. If a life pattern repeats itself, it needs to be addressed or guess what happens? It keeps coming like a boomerang until you say enough is enough and deal with it.

In my early 20's, I began to learn and read about different spiritual paths and various healing modalities. Feeling at times like Tigger (Winnie the Pooh) who couldn't decide what he liked best, wanting to obtain knowledge was like an obsession. I don't know why I was compelled to do these things and was not sure where it would lead, but if I was being guided, there must be a reason. I also began to meditate and my heart expanded with love for humanity.

I have a quote by Edgar Cayce that I keep on my cork board. *"The purpose of the heart is to know thyself and to be yourself and yet one with god."*

There were times when I did stop meditating. But something always drew me back. It was the connection to spirit that I missed. It was that feeling of unconditional love that God, source, the divine, universal intelligence, whatever name you wish to call it, I could sense when meditating. As time passed, I realized for my own growth what I needed was to accept unconditional love for myself, and view myself as lovable and worthy, despite my flaws or my perceived imperfections. I certainly know others love me. I know that beyond measure. I needed to see myself as perfect just the way I am.

Recently while working at the after-school program, I had a five-year-old tell me I was beautiful. She, of course, made my day! She did not see my wrinkles or my arthritic hands. She saw me as whole and complete. It is how we all should see ourselves: perfect inside and out, beacons of light and love.

I learned to connect with loved ones who have passed into the spirit and receive messages from the angelic realm. My view of the universe expanded and I knew there was more to life than washing floors and working at a job I didn't like.

The angels will not interfere in our lives unless asked. They would like to build relationships with us from the other side. Everyone has the ability to receive messages and intuitive insights if you desire. They want you to know this. It is through focused intention, we ask and we do receive. Maybe not in expected ways. It may not be through words you hear being whispered. It could be a conversation with someone, a paragraph in a book that's inspirational, body sensations that indicate you are on the right track. It's tuning in and paying attention. We are always surrounded by angels and loved ones.

I like to have chats with my peeps (those in spirit) in the car, talking aloud while driving, especially if something is bothering me. Other drivers may think I am on a speaker phone. They don't know I have a direct line to heaven. Try it sometime. It's very liberating.

When I first started on my spiritual path, there were few people I could share with what I was learning. We could encourage each other and have great talks about what it felt like to be an empath, etc. I also found that as much I wanted to share with others, each of us eventually finds our passion. I wanted my flock to fly with me but gradually I came to see their purpose was different than mine. We all have our own lessons to learn and we can't stop others from moving forward to where they need to go.

I know we all connected and if we open ourselves to that connection, we are never alone. This is not what I thought I would be doing when I was maiden, mother, and now as crone (grandmother). I am being nudged towards furthering my studies as a minster. I never followed tradition and that's just fine – a quiet rebel in my own way.

There have been times when I did receive spontaneous message from spirit. I was urged to share the inspired that message by spirit. It was uncomfortable the first time it happened. A few years ago, I had a water company employee standing in my kitchen testing the tap water. I was sitting at the kitchen table. This man started to talk about the recent, tragic motorcycle accident that took his sister's life. I felt her presence immediately as he was talking. I had to reluctantly tell him I could connect with people who have crossed over and that sister was with us. He didn't make a run for door, as I thought he might. Instead of fear griping me, I allowed the message to flow. He was grateful and comforted by words she wanted him to hear and the love she felt for him.

A couple of weeks ago, as I was having tea with a wonderful friend of mine, she was upset about her health and how that has impacted her life. I could see her guardian angel behind her. This angel wanted me to share a message with my friend, as she so distraught she could not hear it herself. My friend was open and receptive to message and said it exactly what she need to hear.

Most of the time when giving messages from spirit, I still feel insecure and not good enough, even though I have great feedback. Still, I would be hesitant to tell people I just met what I did. Then, I wondered why people weren't knocking at my door. I knew I was stopping my own flow of abundance because of my fears. Self-doubt would creep in and I would ask myself, "Should I take yet another class? That would solve the problem, right?" When someone did ask for a reading, I was hesitant to jump at the chance and say yes right away. Once I sat down and began my connection to spirit, the anxiety would gradually disappear. I can feel, hear, and see spirit. When all my senses are engaged and by the content of the message, I know I have strong link.

"How was I going to get over this?" I kept asking myself. The message that coming back, that I had refused to hear through my meditations, was that I needed to accept myself – my whole self, not what society deemed as okay and acceptable. I was also afraid to say this was not just hobby. It is who I am, not just a slice of my life. I began to ask, "How may I serve each person with love?"

Again, I had no idea how do this. I was in over my head. I wanted to give up and say this was too hard. I should stay small, like the country mouse who would not leave her house. Easier to go unnoticed than be my authentic self.

As I said previous, God pushes you in directions you don't want to go. We all have dreams and aspirations but sometimes detours pop up and travels plans need to be rearranged. I had to do the inner work to uncover my feeling of inadequacy. I knew I had to fully love and accept who I am. I found a well-known female author to be a great inspiration to see myself in a different light.

I went to a business workshop and had to create an elevator speech about what I do. It's a short introduction of yourself, telling a stranger or potential client what your business is. This is what I came up with: "I am multitalented, a wedding officiate, a medium/angel guidance practitioner, and also an after-school supply teacher." I am still working on making this a little shorter. I do wear many hats.

When I have the courage to say it, I am surprised by some people's reactions – not at all negative. It's a big relief for me.

I see myself as a bridge between heaven and earth and I'm here to experience love in all its many forms. I like this little bit in a Bob Marley song, *"One love, one heart, let's get together and feel all right."* Kinda covers it all.

We do feel all right when we are following our bliss and accepting ourselves and one another without judgment. Spreading love to all is a message the world needs to hear right now.

Blessings

Trina Virgin

Trina Virgin is a mother of two and proud grandmother of three, who currently lives in the Guelph area. Since she has developed a case of wanderlust, who knows where she will be in five years. Trina has been on a spiritual journey for many years and learned to connect with loved ones, guides, and the angelic realm. Writing has also become a passion. Trina offers Mediumship and Angel guidance readings.

trinavirgin@hotmail.com

Facebook "Wings of Love"

Chapter 18

The Healing Power of Passion
by Mary Lynn Stevenson

Love comes in many different forms. It can be the love of another person, a pet, even having learned to love one's self. But love can also be a passion for a sport, music, or art in any form.

I am an artist! It has taken me a long time to embrace and celebrate this wonderful gift I was given at birth.

Growing up, all I wanted was to be an artist; however it was discouraged at every turn. Too many starving artists, you know! So, in high school I took business courses. My creative spirit was locked away deep inside thinking she would never see the light of day again. Over the years, she would try to escape, always being tucked away again. She was hidden out of fear and lack of confidence. Logic would overtake "What am I going to do with all these paintings?"

However, that love of being creative just wouldn't go away. One day she was allowed out in all her glory. And it felt so good to paint again. I felt alive! All my emotions poured out in my artwork. People were drawn to them as they could sense the energy and the emotions. They could feel a part of themselves within these pieces of art.

If you are lucky enough to find your passion, don't ignore it out of fear or lack of confidence. Instead, embrace it! Celebrate that aspiration! Working with your passion is a wonderful way to heal and will add years to your life.

Lynn Stevenson's background has revolved around the music industry, the paranormal, and print media. Aside from being the subject of articles and interviews, she has also been the host of her own radio and television shows, as well as a regular columnist and guest in various media outlets.

www.marylynn@marylynnstevenson.com

Chapter 19

My Little Girl
by Candace Hawkshaw

I have been in and out of romantic relationships. To be honest, I have a hard time because I fall deep and fast into love. Thoughts would run through my mind. "If I show you who I really am, will you truly love me? Will you leave me? When will you go? Candace, why do you run?"

I began to question why I would be having these thoughts with each new person. I realized if I was ever going to have a healthy balanced relationship in my life, I really needed to understand and heal this part of myself. As a healer, I knew that in order for me to do this, I had to go deep within. Once I sat in silent meditation, I asked to be shown the part of me that was causing these fears of loss. What appeared was a little girl hiding deep inside of me.

I was three years old, and I was happy. I had four older brothers and one older sister. Life was filled with joy and innocence. Then one day, my brother Larry, who was the youngest of my brothers, was gone. All I remember as a child was my family talking, and crying. I never saw my brother again. From that day on, all I knew was that everything changed in my life. I may have not known it then, but I know now that I had held onto my family's pain and hurt. I was an empath at that age. I was a good girl and always tried to make my family laugh. I knew something was different, but where was my brother, my playmate, whom I loved?

My life went on, and living in the country on a farm was great. It was the best way to grow up, and I am so grateful for the life skills I learned.

Understanding how to grow our own vegetables, preserve food, and raise animals for meat taught me how to be self-sustaining. I learned how to respect others and the land. We all worked together as a family to keep food on our table. My parents sacrificed a lot to give us special times to enjoy. I remember Christmas with the gifts flowing under the tree and the wonderful memories of the traditional baking my sisters and I did together with my mom. We also did a lot of traveling and camping together as a family when we were older, which opened me up to a whole new world of possibilities.

After high school, I did the same as everyone else: I got married and had kids. I thought I was happy, but I still had this sadness inside, even though I never let anyone see or know it because at that time I did not understand it myself. Recently when I started into a new relationship after six years of being alone, my fears showed up again. Would this person leave like all the rest? Would he truly love me? That was when I began to look deep inside to heal and break the cycle.

I realized the sudden loss of my brother had been imprinted into my younger self, and I believed that people you love just disappear. That three-year-old little girl was still there protecting my heart from pain and hurt, not trusting a lot of people, and wondering if they would disappear too. When anyone gets too close, she builds a wall around my heart. I test the people in my life to see if they will they stay or they will go.

I kept a lot of my feelings and truths shut inside me in fear of abandonment, or making people cry. I needed everyone to like me, and I did things for people so they would.

Now, having this awareness, I am on a mission to heal my little girl who truly is an amazing person, who loves to laugh, play, and bring joy to so many. I am healing my little girl with love and gratitude. I hold her in my arms and tell her she is safe and so loved. I know my brother's spirit is always with me. He was with me for every car accident and my near-death experience. I know and feel his love with me.

Most recently, I once again fell quickly and deeply in Love. I feel that I attracted this person through my manifestation of my true love. I felt so alive, like a light bulb, so bright and so light. That vibration of love was amazing. Then, I ran fast – so fast. I ran without communicating with this person about what was going on in my heart, and in my head. Was I afraid that this man would really see who I was? Would he leave me? Was he letting me see who he really was?

When I finally became aware that my little girl had once again protected me, this was an opportunity to work on my fears. I asked this man to come and hold a safe place for me to speak my truth and face those fears with love. The speaking of my truth would be a huge shift for me on all levels. I have always held back speaking my real deep truth in fear of loss, hurting someone, or abandonment. This step affirmed that my little girl inside was truly ready to come out and take down the blocks of fear through love in order to heal.

Once I was aware of the cycles that kept repeating, I started reprogramming my thought forms about myself. Standing in love for myself has helped me to show my vulnerability and to share my deep feelings. I am learning that friendship love is the best way for me to trust and love deeply without fear.

I now have a sense of joy and excitement because I understand where my sadness, my fear of loss, and my apprehension of sharing my deepest feelings with someone. I am excited for what my future holds. The love for myself, and the love of family and friends helps me get through anything. My heart has expanded with this awareness. I am ready to share this friendship of love. My heart has not broken…it has opened.

I am no longer afraid of loss or abandonment, or to show my vulnerability. I now walk through my fears with love. I am love, and I love myself. I am a light. I do not fear love. I am going to dive deep into the depths of love. I am grateful for that more than ever.

Love never dies. Love carries on forever. I am learning not to run, and to move forward in love. Going into love and seeing what happens, love cannot hurt me, it can heal me. Love given freely without expectations can only grow and blossom. Love is expansive, and can only grow if we detach from what we think our love for someone is, and how it should be. We cannot put love in a box and categorize it. There is no limit to love.

Candace Hawkshaw is a certified Holy Fire II Reiki Master, a teacher, a healer, and a mentor. She is certified in many other complementary healing modalities, and is the bridge that will connect your Soul and Spirit to the Universal Source. Candace is a weaver of Love, who will assist you on your journey to remember who you are and your purpose!! Her business is called Know Thyself. She is an international teacher. Candace has written her stories in three books: The Ruby Red Shoes – Empowering Stories on Relationships, Intuition & Purpose, Living Without Limitations – Vision Quest, & #Peace – A New Perspective of Hope.

http://www.know-thyself.ca

https://www.facebook.com/candacenhawkshaw/

CONCLUSION

Thank you for reading Love Heals - Stories of Love's Healing Journeys.

When I first thought of this anthology, I truly wanted people to know that love really can heal. Loving one's self is the best place to start.

As you have read the stories in this book, you have seen how love actually is the powerful energy that can help heal in any life event or events. Sincerely feeling and knowing love can bring peace and understanding to your life.

The co-authors are all people I know and some are even my Reiki students who found more love when they learned this healing modality. For most of the coauthors, this is their first time writing and actually sharing some very intimate feelings and stories in their lives. I'm so proud to have shared this journey with all of them, and I look forward to hearing all the wonderful feedbacks from family and friends about their book.

During this process, I learned so much about myself, the co-authors, and Love.

If you feel that this book could help someone, please pass it on. I hope that some of the stories will have inspired you or will have given you some hope in your own life, or someone you know.

Love is powerful! Feel Love flow through you and around you. Allow Love to come into your life.

Wishing you Infinite Blessings, Love and Hugs

Candace

I AM a Weaver of Love

Vision Two:

Keep Calm and Live your Empowered Life

ACKNOWLEDGMENTS

I would like to express my gratitude to the many people who saw me through this book – to all those who provided support, talked things over, read, wrote, offered comments, allowed me to quote their remarks, and assisted in the editing, proofreading, and design.

I would like to thank my publisher, Anita Sechesky, and LWL PUBLISHING HOUSE for enabling myself and Candace Hawkshaw to come together as co-compilers in making this book possible. Above all, I want to thank my family for all their encouragement and everyone who supported and inspired me in spite of all the time it took me away from them. It was a long journey for many involved, and as they say…it was not easy but it will be worth it.

Thanks to the best co-authors anyone could have ever asked for, in no particular order: Lisa Berry, Regina Neal, Charise Morris, Tina Gaisin, Laurentino Uscanga, Allan Pollett, Rose Nixon, Michelle Carter, Veronica Hislop, Ana Marie Gonzales Agojo, Janine Berridge-Paul, Lori Canlas-De Pala, Barbara Finlay, and Amna Malik. Without your belief, trust and faith in me, this book would not be possible. Congratulations to all.

Last and not least: I ask forgiveness to all those who have been with me through the years and whose names I have failed to mention here.

DEDICATION

This book is made possible by the love and support of my family: my husband Guy and my son Daniel. I love you both so much. Because of what I want for us as a family, it has done nothing more but empowered me to persevere. Thank you.

VISION TWO
INTRODUCTION

I want to take this time to thank my co-authors for wanting to share their stories of how they have evolved to a life of empowerment and for sharing their triumph of going from pain to healing. This book project is all about giving you the reader a glimpse of what they have gone through, but really and truly focusing on who they are and what helped them to evolve into the Empowered Soul that they have become. They will be giving you, the reader, golden nuggets on how they healed, thereby helping you to heal. They will become your heroes as we take this journey together to live YOUR empowered Life.

Section One:

Stories of Self-Empowerment

It took me quite a long time to develop a voice, and now that I have it, I am not going to be silent. — Madeleine Albright

Ahh! The miracle of Self-Empowerment! It's the moment when you realize that the only way you can make changes is by doing something about it yourself. That's right; you have the power to fix it. It's your world and you can make it better.

You can literally wake up one day and choose to make a change for the better. You can make the choice to take action, which could mean saying something or doing something you've never done or said before. It could be a big thing or something small, but when you make a move there will be an equal or greater reaction. With just one move, you can start the wheel rolling.

Journey with us as we take you to places you have never been before. Learn about the strength of a woman; how she kept going to school even if she had no food for lunch; how she survived cancer four times but kept going so she could support her children to be the best mom she could possibly be. Receive strength from a young mom who had to get out of her abusive relationship and put up with an abusive employer so she could take care of her family.

The amazing stories in this section are about making the change that took courage, strength, and faith. It's real people making real change.

Come read and be inspired by their boldness, self-empowerment, and commitment to make a difference no matter what struggles they faced. Ask yourself, "What would I have done?" or "What should I do to empower myself?" Then say, "If they can do it, so can I!"

Andrea Lavallee

Empowerment Awareness Life Coach, Author, Reiki Master

Chapter 20

Phoenix Rising
by Charise Morris

It was only supposed to be temporary. It was a great opportunity; a gift really. I was ecstatic and grateful for the chance to work in a steady job while I figured myself out. I'd dabbled in college, but the design course I'd taken had not panned out for me. When I got a position at a local factory, I felt like I had won the lottery. I walked around with a silly grin on my face for months. The day I had my picture taken for my plant ID, the photographer said I was the happiest employee she had ever seen. The new-found financial stability made it easy to fantasize about my future. I thought I'd work in the factory, create a solid plan for my future, and save more than enough money to make it all happen. But something went wrong. I got stuck.

The money was easy enough to make at first. The job was predictable. Not much was expected of me other than I was required to be punctual, productive, and obedient. I wasn't allowed to deviate from the system. The described manufacturing process was to be followed in exactly the same order every time it was completed. It was boring but I was alright with that. Eventually, the novelty of the job wore off and the reality of my situation set in: the perfect control I thought I had over my future was an illusion.

When it began poisoning my life, it became clear that the job was a wolf in sheep's clothing. The pain and suffering inflicted through the repetitive movements caused physical injuries to accumulate at a staggering rate. There was also a constant onslaught of emotional abuse. Many of the supervisors were extremely abusive and took pride in their ability to break the weak-minded. They bragged about it. The daily barrage of sadistic head-games took its toll and my happiness started to fade.

Along with the years of abuse I endured at the hands of management, my small frame and gentle voice made me a target for my coworkers on the shop floor. The depraved found me an interesting challenge; my innocent appearance was deceptive. I looked like an easy target but I was surprisingly resilient. One man was especially brutal. He told me he wanted to corrupt me. At one point, he threatened to kill me because I had red hair. Declaring it was his duty to cleanse the world of my evil presence, he used Bible verse to back his claim that my red hair was a sign that I had been touched by the devil. In great detail, he described how I would eventually succumb to death at his hands. Afraid for my life, I asked management and the human right's rep for help but was told they couldn't protect me. Being young, I thought I had done everything possible to make the torture end so when the man laughed in my face and told me I couldn't stop him, I believed him. I cried myself to sleep every night for nine months. Just before I became a target for this man, I'd bought myself a nice little house. I had started dreaming of the day I would one day hear the laughter of my future children playing in the yard. That dream gave me the strength to keep going, so day after day I would swipe myself into the plant and put on my game face.

Eventually, like a snake, the rancor coiled around me. It slowly began squeezing the happiness out of me. My will, motivation, and most importantly, my light was all crushed. I was dying a slow and agonizing death in the vice-like grip of the job; everything that made me unique was slipping away from me. My essence was being replaced with a morbid void; a gaping hole in the depth of my soul and I was sliding downward in a spiral of turmoil and depression. For the first time in my life, I was afraid of myself.

Over the years, I had tried to redefine my path. I took college courses in an attempt to uncover my destiny; hoping to figure out what direction to steer my career. Physics. Accounting. Nursing. Marketing. Nothing sparked my desire. By this point, my desperation to escape the job became so palpable and thick that I'm surprised I didn't choke on it. No matter what avenue I took, I hit dead ends. It seemed the job had finally done what it set out to do. Like the dying embers of a fire, I was virtually gone.

Six years after I officially started as a full-time employee, I had my first child. She was a product of an abusive relationship. I wanted to give her a safe and loving home but I knew that if I stayed with her father, she would endure too much pain. Hurting my baby was not an option for me, so I had one choice: for my daughter's sake, I left. My ex was angry because he had lost control over me. He vowed to financially ruin me and tried to make me go crazy in a failed attempt to portray me as an unsuitable mother. He underestimated me, though, and his efforts backfired. They didn't quell the newly lit flames in my heart like he had hoped; rather they acted like a poker and helped me fight harder. For the first time in years, I had a real purpose: protecting my daughter. She saved me from myself and gave me the courage to walk away from a life of abuse and neglect. Two weeks after her birth, I hired a lawyer and became embroiled in a legal battle over custody of my daughter. I was unable to focus on anything except fighting for her safety. Financially, I was barely making ends meet. My legal expenses kept climbing, accumulating at such a fast pace that I was unable to keep up. With the expertise of a circus clown, I became adept at juggling my creditors. I'd talked my way into re-payment plans and no interest options. Almost three years after it began, I was the victor. I came out stronger and wiser. Broke maybe, but no longer broken. It was time to rebuild my crumbled finances before I could again focus on myself. I put my head down and dug in at work.

Somewhere during this time, I'd stumbled into a loving relationship with a great man. Focused on building my family with him, I was blessed with two more children. The birth of each child brought me such joy and peace. Their very existence covered me in a cascade of healing light that partially rejuvenated my darkened soul, but a part of me was still drowning. I couldn't understand how I could be so happy, yet still feel incomplete.

Spurred by my desire to provide the happiest home for my family, I began looking for answers. Somehow, I eventually figured it out. I finally understood that in order to be complete, I needed to nurture all the dreams of my soul and that included fulfilling the need to have a career with purpose. Before I could find my true destiny, I needed to believe I was worthy of receiving it – not only as a mother and wife, but worthy as an individual.

It should have been a simple task, but I'd spent my entire life believing I was trash. For me, the hardest part about my journey was accepting that I have value as a person. When I looked at myself, I saw flaws. I saw someone who deserved all the abuse and heartache she received. Thankfully, my beautiful children disagreed with me. When they looked at me, they saw beauty and worth. They saw someone deserving and valuable. Their unfaltering belief in me was contagious and the more time I spent encompassed in their unconditional love, the better I felt. Slowly I fell victim to their logic and I started seeing myself through their loving eyes.

With the end of my last maternity leave looming, a familiar feeling began creeping back into my heart: dread. It was different this time; it wasn't all consuming. I had changed. I had finally accepted that I had value as an individual. As soon as I acknowledged my self-worth, everything started falling into place. Like magic, opportunities started manifesting in my life. Amazingly, my outlook toward my job changed and at long last I saw it for what it was: a source of income while I transitioned to a new career.

All the pain I've experienced has made me realize that I want to help heal people. I have started training as an energy healer and my goal is to work with children. I may not know exactly where I'll end up yet, but I know I'm heading in the right direction and it feels wonderful. Like a phoenix rises from the ashes, I too will rise from the trauma of my past.

Charise Morris is a Certified Reiki Practitioner, an entrepreneur, and student of the Universe. She is completing her Usui Reiki Level 2. Her greatest accomplishment to date is being a mom to three beautiful children. Charise lives in Ontario, Canada, enjoys traveling, walks on the beach, camping, and skiing. She has co-authored in a Multi-Vision Anthology, appearing in the *Keep Calm & Live Your Empowered Life* section. By contributing her story, she has fulfilled a lifelong dream of becoming a published author. Charise is the Team Leader for the topic of FINANCES in her next publication coming out this Fall of 2017.

www.facebook.com/charise.morris

sayhellotocharise@hotmail.com

Empower Boost

Growing up Tina
by Tina Gaisin

Growing up, I never thought I was going to have cancer and survive it! I wanted to be a doctor, a wife, a great mother, daughter, and granddaughter! I wanted to be a great person and heal the world back to health and love!

My aspirations never came true though. My marriage of thirteen plus years did not make it and my four young kids at the time did not come out unscathed. And for that, I feel terrible!

My health issues started with me getting very ill and losing a lot of weight! I actually had lots of people tell me how great I looked but I felt worse and worse until I had to go to the hospital! Two blood transfusions and many tests later I was put on bed rest and medicated until I could have surgery! The hardest part was that they were fattening me up so my less than 80 pounds became 140 pounds, and walking was a chore!

I had the first surgery of the year in 2001 after the holidays and for the pain they gave me my morphine drip, which I could pump myself! I had given myself too much and had a near death experience after hearing that I had two types of cancer, but they got everything in the surgery and I would be fine! After all, I had four young kids who were depending on me!

Later that year with my marriage broken, my husband and I split up and the kids were shuttled back and forth! It took me a long time to realize that I was still a good person but I hurt inside and I had to show the world a strong outside! I took comfort in my Jewish identity and religion.

My quest took a long time with many wrong turns along the way! There were a lot great people in my life who appeared and became lifelong friends and there were people who just stopped by for a brief time! I realized that there is a higher purpose and that I am loved! I had two more cancers and got through them (I have lots of scars to prove it). I am a survivor, do keynote speeches, and speak to groups about my experiences!

Do not take anything or anyone for granted! The most important things I learned are the power of women helping women, the power of prayer, and being true to yourself! Listen to the voice that tells you right from wrong and be part of a community! I have a mission – it has always been helping others! I am not a doctor but I help others to reach their potential. Please join me on this fabulous trip!

Tina Gaisin is a mother of four wonderful children, a stepmom, and a soon-to-be mother-in-law! She is a four plus cancer survivor and has a passion for sailing, swimming, and learning. Tina is a b'aalshuva frum lady who has the most wonderful partner in life to share her experiences with and a deep-routed love of HaShem!

tinagaisin@yahoo.ca

Chapter 21

Meditations to Empower Your Soul

by Andrea Lavallee

Dear reader, please feel free to record these and use for meditation and relaxation.

1. Relaxation Meditation

For this meditation, you can choose to sit or lie down. Make sure that you will not be interrupted for the next ten minutes. Turn off your phone and dim the lights – this is your time. You have nowhere to go and nothing to do.

I invite you to close your eyes, rest your hands loosely on your lap or at your side. Now take a long slow deep inhale, in through your nose, then slowly exhale through your mouth, allow any tension that you have to just melt away…that's right.

I invite you to fully relax your entire body. Relax your head…relax your eyes…relax your forehead…relax your cheeks…relax your lips… your neck…shoulders…back…stomach…your legs…toes…arms and fingers…just relax and let go of all tensions…feel your body melt into the relaxation. You are comfortable, peaceful, and relaxed.

Pause

Now it's time to leave the external world behind and go on a relaxing inner journey…a journey to a place of deep inner stillness.

As I count down from ten, you will begin to feel yourself slipping deeper and deeper into a state of complete relaxation 10: just relax now; 9 – 8: feel yourself become more and more relaxed, 7 – 6 – 5: even more relaxed; 4 – 3: just let go; 2 – 1: you are feeling completely safe and completely relaxed.

Pause

You are now taking a walk on the beach, you can hear the seagulls and the ocean waves, there is a cool breeze and the smell of the ocean is in the air. You happen to look to your right and you see a path you feel drawn to it, you decide you need to explore where this path will take you.

You notice the path leads to a forest. You have now entered this forest… you suddenly feel great as the cool breeze blows. You notice a strong tall tree with the leaves waving in the cool breeze as if welcoming you. How does the breeze feel to you? Is it Relaxing? Does it make you want to sit in the shade and day dream?

You now decide to take a rest from all the excitement of your new discovery. You are now sitting on the soft green grass under the tree and the glowing sun is warming your face and body, making you feel even more relaxed. You take the deepest breath of relaxation as you let go of your last bit of tension and you feel good as you watch the clouds go by. Do you see any shapes in the clouds? What shapes do you see?

You start to drift off to sleep and while in a dream state, you see a more relaxed you. The relaxed you that you desire to become. You have messages for yourself. The messages are affirmation for success:

- I am at peace with myself and the universe.
- I am stress free and relaxed in knowing all things will work out for the best.
- I am free from all concerns about the past.
- I am free from all concerns about the future.
- My life is in perfect order and is free from all the stress that limits me from living a carefree life.
- I simply allow my desires to flow to me, and I release my grip on life.
- I am calm in the knowledge that all my needs are taken care of.

- I am vibrant, filled with vitality and life.

- My thoughts are always positive and I am getting positive results; I no longer limit myself from living a full life.

- I am in control of my life and no longer feel life is in control of me.

- I love life and all the gifts that it has to offer.

- I am now living my best life ever.

Pause

You wake up feeling even more alive and completely relaxed to be you and filled with abundance, knowing that you can accomplish anything.

What other feelings are you having right now?

Pause

You now realize you need to get back. You start to walk back and you've found the path that took you to the forest. As I count to five, you will become fully awake and fully alert.

1 – You are back on the path.

2 – You are getting closer. You can hear the sounds of seagulls and the ocean's waves splashing against the rocks.

3 – You reached the end of the trail.

Pause

4 – You are back on the beach. You are feeling clear, calm, and at peace with yourself.

5 – You are fully awake now becoming aware of the sounds in the room. You can wiggle your fingers, and toes, and when you are ready, open your eyes.

2. **Afformations for success**

   Afformations are based on the principle of asking the right questions to get the right results. This is founded on the concept that your mind will never make a liar out of you, so when you ask "Why" questions, your brain will find a way to convince you of its truth. Therefore, results will find their way to you. With this meditation, you ask each question with strong emotions and strong matching feelings.

Begin by declaring these: I am ready for a new beginning and I now accept more success into my life. I now affirm my desires for success. I am ready to ask the right questions so I can become who I really am.

As you say these afformations, I want you to sense what it feels like to know what you are asking is true Try not to answer the questions, but to **feel** the answers. Take notice of which ones resonate with you and repeat throughout the day.

1. Why am I so happy?
2. Why am I so grateful?
3. Why do I love life so much?
4. Why do good things always happen to me?
5. Why do I feel so good?
6. Why do I feel like I can do anything?
7. Why do things come to me so easily?
8. Why am I so abundant?
9. Why do I love my life?
10. Why am I in control of my life?
11. Why do I feel so accomplished?
12. Why am I able to accomplish so much in a single day?
13. Why do I always find what I seek?
14. Why am I so energized?
15. Why am I so good at meeting the right people?
16. Why am I smiling all the time?
17. Why am I so rich?
18. Why am I so loving?
19. Why am I so relaxed?

20. Why does money come to me so easily?
21. Why am I so healthy?
22. Why do I seem to always be in the right place at the right time?
23. Why am I so loved?
24. Why am I so forgiven of myself?
25. Why am I so intelligent?
26. Why do good things always happen to me?
27. Why am I so blessed?
28. Why do I love to help others accomplish their goals?
29. Why am I always so clear about my goals and what I want for mysef?
30. Why am I so confident?
31. Why am I so amazing just the way I am?
32. Why do things flow my way with such ease and grace?
33. Why do I take such good care of myself?
34. Why is life so good to me?
35. Why am I always on time?
36. Why am I so lucky?
37. Why am I so special?
38. Why am I so good at everything I set my mind to?
39. Why am I so good at manifesting my dreams?
40. Why am I so awesome?
41. Why am I so talented?
42. Why am I so focused?
43. Why do I always get the results I seek?
44. Why am I so patient?

45. Why am I so intelligent?

46. Why am I so full of life?

47. Why am I so happy to be me?

48. Why do I always reach my goals?

49. Why am I so successful?

And so it is.

3. **Guided meditation for success**

   For this meditation, I have incorporated a NLP technique called Goal Getting Process.

   You can choose to sit or lie down. Make sure that you will not be interrupted for the next ten minutes. Turn off your phone and dim the lights – this is your time. You have nowhere to go and nothing to do.

   I invite you to close your eyes, rest your hands loosely on your lap or at your side. Now take a long slow deep inhale, in through your nose, then slowly exhale through your mouth, allow any tension that you have to just melt away…that's right.

   I invite you to fully relax your entire body. Relax your head…relax your eyes…relax your forehead…relax your cheeks…relax your lips… your neck…shoulders…back…stomach…your legs…toes…arms and fingers…just relax and let go of all tensions…feel your body melt into the relaxation. You are comfortable, peaceful, and relaxed.

   Pause

   It is a short time from now and as you look back on your life, you realize how far you have come…and how happy you are that you did not give up the hope that you would get this far…you have now found success for yourself…you have accomplished all your dreams and have met all your goals. What was that goal? Was it financial freedom? A new car? Was it that your business receives the recognition that it so deserves? Was it to lose weight? Perhaps a happier family relationship or better health? Whatever it was, you made it? How does it feel? Amazing? Outstanding? Fantastic? That's right, all of the above. In a short time from now, you see yourself looking at your accomplishments…take it all in now. What are you wearing?…what day is it?…where are you right now?…are you sitting or standing?…

what sounds do you hear?...how do you feel?

Pinch yourself because it must be a dream...no, it's not a dream at all. You felt that pinch, didn't you...that's because its real. You did it. You made it happen...others didn't believe you at times, but you did. Others thought you needed a reality check, but you knew what you were doing all along. That's right, it was not easy but it was worth it. What is your new title...founder, creator, CEO...stay at home mom?... how about just happy?

First you set your intention on what you wanted for yourself, then you focused on it with intensity and power.

And then you waited for it to come in and it was all because you believed. Who else is happy for you? Your children, your spouse, your community? How does it feel to see them so happy for you?

Day in and day out, you trusted in the process that you would get your heart's desire and now you got it and it's better than you have ever imaged. It suits you and you can't stop smiling. And so it is...

When you are ready, you will begin to begin to hear sounds in the room that you are in and you will become fully awake. You can stretch, wiggle your fingers and toes, and when you are ready, open your eyes.

Andrea Lavallee is an Empowerment Awareness Consultant and Life Coach. She is the founder of The Empowerment Coaching Group, and the host of the International radio show, The Life Coach Radio Show, which broadcasts about connecting with Life Coaches and empowering the audience. Andrea is a Reiki Master Instructor, Certified Life Coach, NLP Certified Practitioner, Author, and Speaker. Andrea has a BA in psychology and had been empowering people for over fifteen years in the social services field before making to jump to Life Coaching and Reiki. Andrea is available for live speaking opportunities, in person workshops, and one-on-one coaching.

https://www.facebook.com/empowermentcoachingbyandrea

Alavallee2008@gmail.com

Empower Boost

Beautiful Sorrow
by Charise Morris

Having my baby felt like a double-edged sword. On the one hand, it was the best decision I had ever made. The love I had for my daughter was unconditional and all-consuming. The moment she was placed in my arms, she became my reason. She was my purpose and my only love. On the other hand, I had brought her into a mess. Her birth could have forever united two families, but instead it divided us. The conflict and turmoil in my life was overwhelming. Soon after her birth, I was immersed in a custody battle and my every action was criticized. The pressure was tremendous.

I sat alone one night after I had put my tiny baby to sleep. I was suddenly struck by the memory of myself as a child, dreaming about my future life. In that dream, I was married to my soul mate and we had created a loving home in which to raise my imagined children. I was instantly filled with regret because this was the exact moment when I realized that my childhood dreams would never be fulfilled. I sobbed. The despair was immense. I cried for the child I once was. I wept for my own daughter who had unknowingly been dragged into the mess I had created. She would be the one to suffer the most pain. Leaving my ex was a necessity, but I was wrought with guilt about it none-the-less.

Almost eight years after that night, I look back on that moment. I can still clearly see it and if I let myself wallow in that pain, I can feel the anguish. The failure. The regret. I can almost taste the salty tears as they rolled down my cheeks. The pain from that one moment was so enormous that

I doubt I will ever forget it.

While I sat consumed in my sorrow, I lost myself. A part of me died that night and in one of the darkest minutes of my life, I became nothing. In becoming nothing, I opened myself up to endless possibilities, and through the years of the highs and the lows, I have found my courage. I discovered my strength. I started becoming the person I was meant to be, on the path toward living the life I was supposed to live.

Without my beautiful sorrow, I wouldn't be living my most magnificent life. The birth of my daughter was wholly miraculous in more than the typical way because she instigated my own profound transformation. My changes lead me to my soul mate. We have a gorgeous family. I have peace and love and am cherished. Incredibly, when I became a mother I also gave birth to my own journey of self-discovery.

Charise Morris is blessed with a loving husband and three amazing children. She believes life is enriched through learning and having a lighthearted attitude. Charise enjoys music, great food, and the company of her loved ones. She is grateful for the miracles of everyday life and is passionate about her family.

www.facebook.com/charise.morris

Chapter 22

From Rags to Diamonds
by Ana Marie Gonzales Agojo

There are secrets everyone keeps. The darkest, however, could be found once light has thumped it rays on it. This is heart in control. I have seen myself crawl, heard a bird sing a song. I've sorted right from wrong. It's been a year since I started a new life. After all this time, I think I'm worth a dime. I wished that everything in life was as easy as a magic trick. But I didn't know that, like a magic trick, life could also be deceiving. I exhausted myself in order to achieve the wealth that no one could take away. I learned my lesson the hard way – that money is not the top problem for achieving your dreams.

I am writing this memoir as I have gathered all my strength to share a part of myself. A year ago, there was a very important lesson life taught me. This was not found in any book or in any imagined internet engine. It is a lesson that taught me how to discern, sacrifice, and save every penny that you have.

Let's see it straight. Let me make it clear where I am coming from. I am a fruit of love of two wonderful people. I am the first child and the eldest daughter of my Mama and Papa. I also have two beautiful sisters. I am also proud to say that I am a grandma's girl. My grandmother used to help my parents take care of me when I was a little child. My mother worked in a city at that time, which was a three-hour bus ride from the province where we lived. For that reason, my mother chose to come home every weekend. It was hard for a mother like her to live far away from her daughter, but because she wanted to meet my needs, she endured working far away from us. My father was working in another country at that time and tried his luck to find a job with a good salary. Unfortunately, his employer didn't pay enough salary. After a year, he came back home and found another job here.

I was two years old when my mother got pregnant with my younger sister. Then, after giving birth to my younger sister, the following year my youngest sister also was born. I was three years old then, when my grandmother was diagnosed with diabetes. After that, my mother decided to resign from her work because my grandmother couldn't take care of us anymore. With the small amount of money that my father earned as a construction worker, we tried to survive. We experienced eating one can of sardines between five members of the family. Sometimes, we ate rice and poured a cup of coffee because we don't have anything else to eat. I remember my mother's facial expression every time we are hungry and she had nothing to give to us. So, I am telling you this to "Be thankful if you can eat three times a day. And be thankful that your tummy is full!" I can also recall the time that I saw my mother hiding in a corner of our house and crying just because she noticed that we kept our eyes glancing to a kid who had delicious food and drinks in his hands as he passed in a front of our house. To those parents, I might say that a child must know the essence of kindness. Teach them how to give and share, even in a simple way, at their young age.

I was at the age of five when I start to go to school as a kindergarten pupil. I can't forget my first day of school. I walked from our home with my Mama. I didn't have a school bus service so I walked. After the flag raising, Mama left me in our classroom and would pick me up after class because she needed to earn money for our daily needs. During recess time, I got confused because some pupils went out the door to bring in their food. However, my mother forgot to give me money for my snacks or she forgot to pack my snacks for me. My teacher asked me why I wasn't eating, and then she gave me some soup. I can still recall those time that I only had one notebook, one pad of paper, one pencil, a small eraser, and crayons with eight colors in my bag. Those times, I always prayed that I would also own more notebooks, a pencil with a different length, a longer eraser like a size of hotdog, and crayons with many, many colors.

During my elementary days, I only had a few friends. Who would dare to make friends with a little girl who only went to school wearing slippers or flip-flops; who only had two blue skirts and two white tops for her school uniform? It was never a hindrance to me. Instead it made me stronger to face the criticism that I got. I knew how proud my parents were that I was learning on my own. I learned how to write without any help from my parents. I also remember those times that my classmates were playing in a playground and I chose to stay inside our classroom to read our books. I love reading and I'm sad about how some people do not read at all. I felt like a firefighter hosing down my classmates with ideas about reading. Often times, however, I would feel all dry because only a few would show enthusiasm about reading. During those childhood times, I didn't have any beautiful toys. Sometimes, I was sewing just to earn a small amount.

I used to be a top achiever of our class. However, I'm sad to say that I couldn't belong to the overall honor list due to a very unfair grading system and favourtism from teachers. Yes, you read it right. There was favourtism but I wasn't treated fairly by our teacher. I wasn't from a rich family and I was not gorgeous. I couldn't buy something to give to my teachers, but still I did my best. They didn't always put me in the first section, but I still tried my best. I can still recall those times that I did DIY (Do It Yourself) on my projects just to save and lessen the expenses. I used to teach my younger sisters with their lessons at home. Often times, I also helped them with their school projects or shared my ideas and knowledge with them. There were so many school activities and contests that I couldn't join because of financial issues. And because of this, I couldn't get extra points on my grades. What I could do was to study well, cooperate during recitation, and get a high score during exams. I was a grade IV when I started to write a journal. I also joined the school publication when I was a grade V student. I made an extra effort and shared my opinions on news writings. I also joined a competition and for a position in editorial writing. Because of the effort that I did, I graduated with an honor when I was grade VI. I received an award of third honorable mention. My father started working abroad at that time and I knew how he was so proud of me.

High school life became more challenging to me. I went to a public school and it was good to become a part of the first five section. Most of my classmates were brainy. It was a sacrifice to wake up early in the morning and wait beside the street for a Jeepney to travel to school in before or exactly at 5:00 am. I cried a bucket of tears as I stepped into high school. Despite all this, I became strong and showed them that I could do it. I always went to school, even with a meagre pocket. Some laughed at me because I didn't change my bag and I always wore the same pair of shoes whatever the weather – rain or shine. Yes, during the four years in high school, I only had one pair of shoes and one bag. And for those four years, I walked from school to the Jeepney terminal, going home after my classes. I chose that way to save and sustain the other matters that I needed for my studies, such as projects and other school supplies. All my sacrifices paid off as I still belong to the top achievers of our class.

When I was a first-year college student, I went to one of the prestigious universities in our province, where I took Bachelor of Science in Information

Technology. But because of the high tuition fee and expenses, I knew my parents might be stressed and it was very hard for me to study far away from home. I decided to transfer to the nearest college. Since my course was not available in our college at that time, I decided to shift to a related course: Bachelor of Science in Computer Science. It was not easy for me to take that course but I was always positive and thought "I CAN." I didn't have my own desktop computer or laptop to use in creating computer programs. Just analyzing each task that they gave me and with the help of paper and pen doing pseudo code, using flow charts and algorithm, and spending time reading programming books, I passed my course. At times, they found me at the school Computer laboratory creating programs there. I graduated and pass all my subjects.

After one year, I was hired in one of the leading companies here. And now, I'm doing a home-based job or online marketing, and currently I'm with a circle of wonderful people who have a same advocacy as mine. I always thank God, my parents, my mentors, and all the people behind my success. Always think positive and you can achieve what your heart desires.

Ana Marie Gonzales Agojo is a graduate of Bachelor of Science in Computer Science (Ladderized Program). She was born and raised in Batangas, Philippines along with her two siblings. Her passion for writing began at an early age in elementary school. Ana Marie's story is about her journey pursuing an education despite the many challenges she faced. She is currently secretary of a non-profit organization. She also enjoys promoting tourism, inspiring the youth to gain education, and joining community outreach programs. Ana Marie is now an inspiring entrepreneur and is aiming to start her own business.

E-mail: agojoanamarie@yahoo.com

Skype: agojo.anamarie

Empower Boost

How I Developed Self-Compassion and Learned to Soothe Myself…Instantly
by Veronica Hislop

What do you need to do right now for your own sense of replenishment, well-being, and peace of mind?

This powerful question that I ask myself usually surfaces at a time of distress. It allows me to stop, pause, focus on myself, and become more mindful of what I need to do in that moment to soothe myself.

The day I found my power question was the day I learned to connect to my inner, wiser self. I had woken up one morning in the midst of a panic attack. Weighed down by burdens and responsibilities of caregiving for others, I couldn't breathe. I hadn't even gotten out of bed; I had yet to fully embrace the day, but I was already geared up for a battle with stress. The day hadn't even started and already I was in need of comfort.

Power questions are those conversations that we have with our inner wise mind that allow us to become healers to ourselves. Asking the right question can open up possibilities that we were unaware existed.

Trying to shift from my head to a deeper place within while asking this simple question, I randomly searched and listened quietly to the part of my body that allowed me to feel a sense of kindness and compassion towards myself. Gently placing my hand on different parts of my body, I listened quietly and paid attention to where and when I felt calmer and relaxed. When and where did my body soften, my shoulders drop? Where and when did my breathing slow down?

For some people, it is the cupping of the face or the placing of the hand over the heart that provides the greatest sense of calm; for me it was gently placing my hands on my tummy. Immediately, I began to quiet my brain, release, let go, and go within. It was this powerful question, accompanied by this simple action, that allowed me to find and connect with the compassionate, kinder voice that dwelled within.

The voice of compassion within us is the voice hidden deep inside. It is the voice that infrequently comes to the surface. It is the voice that is often overshadowed by other more powerful and stronger voices such as that of negativity, anger, and fear.

The questions we ask ourselves that highlight our compassion are the questions that allow for reflection, self-awareness, and highlight our need for utmost self-care.

Ask your simple power question…and wait quietly, for the just as simple powerful answer.

Veronica Hislop is a Certified Life-Relationship Coach, with a Masters Degree in Social Work, a BA in Community Development, and renowned "Change Magnate" in her local community. She is a prolific E-Zine author, who describes herself as a "Ninja Stress Buster." You can get her free Power Stress Tool Kit from her website.

www.empowered-solutions.ca

Chapter 23

I Am Living My Empowered Life
by Andrea Lavallee

A better life is what I always wanted for myself and my family. This all started when I discovered that I was an entrepreneur. I didn't know it then, but I sure do know my true life calling now. I attempted everything I could to find financial freedom. I was involved with the majority of the network marketing businesses that seemed to be a good fit, but nothing worked. I wasted a lot of effort, time, and money. However, I am very thankful that I tried. One day, I decided to meet up with a friend for lunch. We chatted about her wanting me to join her business venture. I completely trusted her, but I couldn't see myself joining another network marking company. I wanted to, for once, stay focused on myself and put all my energy into building my current business. As I started to tell her my stories of all the companies I had enthusiastically signed up for, which ultimately ended in defeat, I started to cry out of the frustration these experiences had caused. I had not recognized that all the failures had disappointed me so deeply and these feelings had stayed with me all these years. All of a sudden, she mentioned something I never realized I was doing. She said, "You might have failed, but you never quit. You kept on persevering through all the failures." I was enlightened to the fact that she was right. While I definitely never quit, I kept going and continued searching for my work-life passions.

I learned that the network marketing era was not a huge loss for me. I found that one needs to have a strong focus if one wants to get anywhere in business, and you cannot do that without having passion. I realized I had no passion for those ventures. Fast forward a few months and another network marketer was trying to recruit me, so I told him it looked and sounded great but I must admit I just didn't have any passion for it. He replied, "You don't need passion to do this." I chuckled to myself as I finally recognized that without the right desire, I was going to be wasting my time. But what was my passion? What did I stand for?

It all started when I was in my 40s, my husband was in his 50s, and our son was four. I realized that I was forced to do it all. About three years after returning from maternity leave, I was completely drained. I knew it was time to start finding my purpose and living my dream so that I could have more time for my family and myself.

I had a very stressful, highly demanding job. I had a son who needed a lot of my attention and extra loving care. I had a husband with chronic back pain who did not drive in the city, and we had no family close by to lend a helping hand. A typical day for me started by dropping my son off at school by 7:30 in the morning, followed by catching the train downtown, and then picking my son up after finishing work. Afterwards, I was coming home to make dinner, giving my son his bath, and putting him to bed. However, my day was not over yet because I would stay up past midnight in order to get work done. Somewhere in my full day, I needed to buy groceries and run other errands. On the weekends, I would take my son out so that he was not spending all his time in front of the TV. After returning from a fun and exhausting day, I would start working on assignments for my business before starting dinner. If my husband helped one day with our son's bath and story time, he might not be able to help the next day due to pain and exhaustion from his back issues flaring up or by working his physically demanding job. After being a solo parent for three years, I just couldn't do it anymore. I realized that I had no time for self-care, I was completely exhausted each night, and I was very angry with the extra effort I had to produce each day.

Honestly, I had to do something because I was completely burned out. I had developed anxiety and high blood pressure from my current job as I had been given a negative performance review. I knew what was coming next, so I took control of my own life and quit my job. Well, we all know the saying, "When one door closes, another one opens." There was nothing I wanted more than to do things on my own terms, have more time for myself, and make enough money without the job stress – this was my dream for living my empowered life. The problem was that at the time, I didn't know what I stood for. I didn't even have a voice. I was still traumatized from my negative work experience and all my past failures with network marketing were distracting me from moving forward in business.

I wanted to be able to fully and completely give all my love to my son by spending more time with him. I needed my husband to retire from his strenuous job, I had a passion to help other people do the same, and I wanted to have a career that would allow me to grow as a person while still being a loving mother and attentive, supportive wife to my husband. These were the goals of my dream life.

In the beginning, what I had in mind for my Empowering People business was the complete opposite of how it all turned out. Yet, I am very grateful for what I have learned. I believed that all I needed was to implement SEO (also known as Search Engine Optimization – or giving my website the most exposure it could possibly receive) and my clients would just flock in for information. I thought to myself, "I can just sit behind a computer and write blogs that everyone from all over the world would come to visit. All I need to do is to coach people all day through Skype in my pajamas while getting paid." Besides, I just had to offer a freebie and the people would pour in, right? Well, that didn't happen at all. By then, I was running out of savings and my Employment Benefits were ending soon.

I realized I was not a "sit-behind-the-computer-and-grow-a-business" kind of professional. I needed to be in actual contact with my clients. Even though I did not like speaking in front of others, I did it. I felt that I was terrible at introducing myself at networking events, and that I had nothing to offer my audience. I found myself promoting fertility workshops and fertility coaching programs to grandmothers and old men: talk about depressing. I realized I had to do something about this.

After years of soul-searching, inner-healing, and trying to figure my life out, I appreciated that I had a lot to offer the world. People started to tell me just how powerful I was, but I still didn't understand it. I thought, "Me? Powerful?" I would say to myself, "You have such a long way to go. You have so much more work to do on yourself." However, I still didn't really know what I stood for in my life. I just knew I wanted to empower others, but I didn't know how?

I started to build my tool box of things that made me feel better, because I figured if they worked for me, they could work for others. I discovered Tapping (also known as EFT, which refers to emotional freedom technique, a method used to improve emotional health). I started working on tapping out all the negative energies that had been trapped inside of me. I started attending a lot of conferences and seminars, and it was at these events when I started to meet people just like myself who were experiencing similar life situations. They were entrepreneurs who wanted to give of their skills and talents to build their amazing businesses, and in connecting, I felt like I had come home. I became certified in NLP (neuro-linguistic programming), and learned the ability to shift negative energy using my mind and thoughts, as well as a Reiki Master, learning how to use my hands to build up and raise my vibration. I also enjoyed the power of working with a life coach and how much further I was able to proceed on my own life's journey. I started to embrace the teachings of well-known authors and teachers of holistic and new age theories. While practising sincere fasting and prayer, I wrote an e-book and created a program for women with infertility issues. Through all these new life applications, I started to gain strength and move forward to my ultimate vision and life-goals.

I learned how to connect with people, which lead me to cultivate a huge network of people. They were mostly mentors and people in similar circles with a common vision, who had experienced the same situations with similar interests as I had. Through my contacts and connections, I was able to start a radio show on Blog Talk called "The Life Coach Show" which is about connecting with life coaches and empowering an International audience.

During the years of figuring this out, I went back to the drawing board so many times that I started to feel like the Wile E. Coyote (the Saturday morning cartoon character who never really succeeded in catching his prey). I realized I needed to change things. First, I changed my brand from my original title of Fertility Coach, decided to open up to more people, and brand myself as an Empowerment Coach. I still had a fertility piece to my brand, which made me very pleased with this new era. I added to the foundation of coach training, NLP (neuro-linguistic programming) training, then Reiki training. Finally, I added empowerment workshops, speaker, radio host, and author to my resume. By now, I had self-published an e-book, currently available on Amazon Kindle, called, *"Day 1: 101 Things to Consider on Day 1 of Your Cycle When You are Trying to Conceive."* All the while, the learning and growing kept occurring in both my personal and professional lives.

I love working with my clients and helping them to find their own strengths, voices, and powers within themselves. I now brand myself as an Empowerment Awareness Coach and Consultant, Author, Speaker, and Reiki Master Instructor, and I love it!

Andrea Lavallee is an Empowerment Awareness Consultant and Life Coach. She is the founder of The Empowerment Coaching Group, and the host of the International radio show, The Life Coach Radio Show, which broadcasts about connecting with Life Coaches and empowering the audience. Andrea is a Reiki Master Instructor, Certified Life Coach, NLP Certified Practitioner, Author, and Speaker. Andrea has a BA in psychology and had been empowering people for over fifteen years in the social services field before making to jump to Life Coaching and Reiki. Andrea is available for live speaking opportunities, in person workshops, and one-on-one coaching.

https://www.facebook.com/empowermentcoachingbyandrea

Alavallee2008@gmail.com

Empower Boost

Who Am I?
by Barbara Finlay

I am often asked to write something about myself. It is usually contextual, such as a bio for a speaking engagement or an event program, or even for an online profile. While I can describe myself as a teacher, facilitator, speaker or professional, I am also a sister, aunt, friend, and community member.

I have learned the most about myself when I stay silent and let others give me a descriptive label that I would not immediately have considered.

I'm not talking about negative labels here. We all have enough times in our lives when people can be critical and unfair. It will not come as a surprise that, at times, I can be the source of some of the unkindest labels. I am not alone in this. We can all suffer from being excessive in self-criticism.

While attending a creative writing retreat, the instructor invited me to come to a literary festival that was to be held later in the summer. I enjoyed the event and when I met up with her that day, she introduced me to others as a writer. I had never been called a writer before. Social worker, teacher, and leader, yes, but this new title made me think about myself in a different way.

When facilitating groups, I often "go off topic" to relate an anecdote that I think will underscore my topic. When discussing this tendency to a colleague one day, she said I was a story teller. That made sense to me and it was a description I felt really fit and felt comfortable with. Like it or not, I seem to have a story for any occasion.

Membership on committees and community groups is part of my life and we are often called upon to come up with new ways to do things or solve problems. Creative is the word that is used quite often to describe my contributions to such groups. I am also happy that they use practical as well because ideas alone do not solve problems.

The key to self-awareness and making change in my life was to think outside my narrow perceptions about who I am and to open myself up to other ways to think about who I am. When I am at a crossroads in my life and I question who I am and where I am going (yes this still happens at fifty-eight), I reflect on some of those titles that I have been given.

Contemplating the "names" I carry with me gives me the courage to open myself up and to ask others, "What do you see in me?", and to consider what that means in my life.

and when did my breathing slow down?

Barbara Finlay has been a trainer and coach for twenty-five years. She currently assists small businesses and social enterprises with goal-setting and growth. Spiritual and personal growth are additional workshops topics and she enjoys hearing about the life journeys of others.

https://www.linkedin.com/in/barbara-finlay-758ba6b9

Chapter 24

I Never Wanted to Give up, Ever

by Andrea Lavallee

After moving to Canada in 2001, I only had one goal in mind and that is to live the life of my dreams. I just wanted it to be a stress-free easier life. I was able to find work fairly easily and not long after that, I met my husband, got married, and had a beautiful baby boy, who is the love of my life. I am so grateful that I get to spend time with him and always be there for him.

But it was not that easy.

HOW IT ALL STARTED

I was born and raised in Jamaica and when I was twelve years old, my mom, sister, and I moved to the United States. I learned very quickly that it's not a good feeling to not be trusted, and it's a very hard thing to change someone's feelings about you who does not trust you. But that feeling of being blamed for something you're not guilty of is very difficult and weighed heavily on my soul.

My mom approached me one day and wanted to put me in therapy for not talking. She suspected that her second husband, the man who us to come to America was "sleeping" with me. I was shocked and surprised by her assumption and wondered why she didn't believe me that it was not true.

Growing up, I was afraid of my mom because she would put me down so much. If I sang a song, she would tell me not to sing. If I said something, she would tell me how unambitious I was. So as a sensitive child, who was afraid to speak up, I would not speak around her or share any details. So to tell her that my step-father never laid a hand on me, and to have me go through testing and therapy made me feel like I had no voice of my own.

After I graduated from University

I don't know how but with the Lord's help, I graduated from university. I was not the best student in high school, but I did love school and loved to learn. I got in university on a program for low income families and so neither my mom nor I didn't have to pay any money for my studies. I am so grateful for that. I majored in Psychology and was the first in my family to finish secondary and post-secondary education. After graduating, I think my mom wanted me to stay home and help her financially because when I mustered up the courage to tell her I was moving out, the look on her face and the feel of her energy told me it was not what she was expecting.

But I wanted to live my life, I wanted to feel free, I wanted to talk again. I wanted to feel like I was someone important.

I started to live again

It was not easy; I had a lot of growing up to do. I was in an amazing one year relationship that taught me so much and most importantly that I could be loved. I also learned how to live alone on my own, if you don't count the cats. I didn't really know how to share my feelings or emotions, which was really hard for me, and as I got older and set in my ways, I never really saw it as an issue. I just peg myself as reserve, quiet, and introverted.

I loved connecting with people and good friends. In fact, I learned that I loved deep conversation about the mysteries life.

The trust thing never came up much through my journey but I did learn to be up front and honest with people because I know that's the person I wanted to be. If they did not believe me, it was just a sadness I had to deal with. I never wanted to be misleading, so I just became that person who did not want to share my feelings, speak my truth, or stand in my light.

There needed to be a shift

If you spend a lot of time with yourself, you get to really learn about yourself and so one of the things I learned is that I had a power within myself that needed to come out. I knew I had skills and talents that involved working with people and making them feel empowered.

It all started when I decided to move to Canada in September 2001, within two weeks of 9/11. I drove my 1986 Volvo, with just some cloths, my VCR, and my cat, Jeri, across the Canadian border. The plan was to stay with my grandmother, find work, and get settled.

I was feeling freer than I had ever felt. It was almost as if the further away I was from my mom, the lighter and freer the energy.

The move was a new start, a new beginning. I found work within two weeks related to my field of social services and after one year I found an even better job. The first job made me dislike Canadian employers as I found that I was having a hard time with my employer. She started to make me feel inferior and was again taking my voice away. I wanted out and was able to find work a year later, which was the best job I ever had. I started to like Canadian employers but they weren't as trusting as my American employers. However, I stayed at this job over nine years, I met my husband there, and made lifelong friends. They were like my family, and had no problem writing my sponsorship letter when I needed to renew my work permit. I was allowed to have my voice again. In fact, it was getting stronger and powerful but I learned I was not very confident around people in authority or speaking in large groups, so I still had work to do.

The Turning Point

Ever feel that there are crossroads in your life where you have to make a choice? Well with me, I have noticed that when it's time to make a change, I feel a strong compulsion to do something, a sense of boredom, and Bam! There it is – the opportunity. I wanted a change as I was completely bored with my job, and felt like I needed to be doing something exciting. Plus, I think there was some depression going on as I had miscarried our second child, at eleven weeks gestation, about a year before.

I got a job with the government, and I left my best job of nine years, but I wasn't going to say no to more money and the opportunity to work from home three days per week. It was exactly want I wanted. By then, my son was three and a half, and what mom doesn't want to be close to home with a young child. It was fantastic.

A year and a half went by and that new job bliss was fading away. The nice government job was not it. I was so dissatisfied, and felt "bored" again, until I discovered Life Coaching.

Everything happens for a reason, just wish it didn't have to be so painful

I was now under a new manager and things were not going well. I guess I could say things were going to hell. Yup, you guessed it – she tried taking my voice away. I felt like everything I said was wrong, stupid, did not matter, or not important. I wanted to cry and run away. And I did. I remember crying in the bathroom as I felt sick and tired of being sick and tired. I was not going to let her take my power away, no way. After three months of anxiety, stress, and high blood pressure, I took my power back and quit! Yup, I was not going to let her fire me, no way. It felt so good.

I started to focus on my coach training and business, but I also had a lot of work to do on myself. But I have to say, I have never felt more empowered in my life. I felt so in control of me and was never more needed. I am now able to help others live their empowered life because I never wanted to give up, ever. My journey has helped me to find my purpose. As a coach, I love helping and empowering people and this is what is so exciting. I thank my mom and all those people who tried to take my power away because it only made me stronger and able to connect more with the people I need to be helping. Just recently I was in a meeting with a potential client who was searching for himself. He discussed a bit of his childhood. I shared my story of my mom taking away my voice and he was able to totally relate. He gained insight on the spot. You see, that's what it's about. You are not meant to be quiet if you're able to help others to become someone different, someone better.

My son, who is eight years old now, is the total opposite of me. If he does not like something, he will tell you. He will let you how you're making him feel and why it's not right. I love and respect that so much about him. He already has his voice and isn't allowing anyone to take that away from him. Now don't think I'm here to blame or that I don't like my mom. She did her best with what she had and what she knew to be true. I chose her to be my mom for a reason and I am grateful for her. My life lesson was always to speak up and empower. I needed to lose my power and work to get it back in order to really appreciate having it and keeping it. For that, I am grateful.

Andrea Lavallee is an Empowerment Awareness Consultant and Life Coach. She is the founder of The Empowerment Coaching Group, and the host of the International radio show, The Life Coach Radio Show, which broadcasts about connecting with Life Coaches and empowering the audience. Andrea is a Reiki Master Instructor, Certified Life Coach, NLP Certified Practitioner, Author, and Speaker. Andrea has a BA in psychology and had been empowering people for over fifteen years in the social services field before making to jump to Life Coaching and Reiki. Andrea is available for live speaking opportunities, in person workshops, and one-on-one coaching.

https://www.facebook.com/empowermentcoachingbyandrea

Alavallee2008@gmail.com

Empower Boost

I See My Beauty. I Feel My Power. I Recognize My Worth.
by Rose Nixon

The way we live life, the space we live in, and the things we bring into our living spaces can often leave us feeling overwhelmed and stressed out. It's easy to get lost in all the chaos and clutter, and making heads or tails of it feels impossible.

With the overwhelming feeling of living in chaos, whether cluttered by physical things in your environment or by negative forces in the people that surround you, there comes a time when you want to know what calm sounds likes, what stillness looks like, what centered feels like. Don't get me wrong. I'm not looking to extract the life out of my life. I'm actually looking to inject far more into it.

I spent most of my childhood in chaos and noise, being told what to do, how to feel, and who to be. But somehow, I found ways to drown out a lot of it. It started with reading. I read every day, often reading a novel a day. It was a way to escape. With every page of every book I read I transcended, gaining a powered sense of self-awareness and assuredness. Music and art was next. Creative expression was key for me. I recognized very early on that I was who I was and I was good with that. I experienced ridicule, embarrassment, and abuse from the people who were supposed to love me most. There were times when I even bought into the sell and believed that what was being said to me and what was being done to me was somehow deserving and warranted.

When you are told, as a young girl, that you were "an ugly baby" and that "I don't like girl children," you tend to question your validity. When you're being told this by your mother and she does not hesitate to repeat it to you time and again for the balance of your young life, you have a tendency to internalize the awfulness of it all. She does not know the impact of her words. She does not see her own beauty. She does not love her own femininity. You wish it wasn't so and your heart feels weighted by your soul's sadness for her and for you. I am my mother and my mother is me. So, it cuts deep and it bleeds with a tar-like viscosity that never washes away. As you mature and you grow into your own person with each passing decade and you eventually become a parent to your own children, you realize that God was not a fool. The beauty in their eyes, the sweetness of their faces, lets you know that she absolutely had you, and herself, all wrong. I see my beauty. I feel my power. I recognize my worth. The less chaos I allow into my physical space and into my active life, the more room I create for my calm to sit quietly next to the noise of my power.

Rose Nixon is an award-winning entrepreneur, Principal, and Chief Professional Organizer of ReallyOrganizedNow (RON), an organizing company for home, office, and life. Rose teaches active women, who move and shake the world with their awesomeness, the values of living an organized lifestyle and creating clutter-free functional living spaces.

facebook.com/reallyorganizednow

Chapter 25

Perseverance Is My Only Option
by Janine Berridge-Paul

My story is dedicated to my husband. Thank you for walking through the storm with me from day one when we were fifteen years old. I love you for being you, for loving me past my pain, seeing the true me, and helping me find my voice. I also dedicate this to my mother whose presence and voice I miss every day. You are an inspiration to me. To my father who has supported me through the years and been my mother and father following the loss of my mom, you are the definition of strength. Thank you to my best friends who have inspired me and supported me on my path in this life.

The Beginning

I never knew that trauma you experience from a young age can deeply impact your life so significantly and lead you down a path of self-destructive behavior. I was never the person to outwardly show my suffering, but instead I would hide it, bury it so deep that no one could see the bruises left on my soul from years of unresolved trauma.

It all started when I was fifteen and in high school. The day I met him, my world would be forever changed. Looking back, being in an abusive relationship from that young age completely changes your view of the world around you. No matter how bright your world may actually be, you can't seem to see through the dark cloud that follows you wherever you are. This cloud follows you to the mall, follows you on a walk, while you read, while you sleep, through every breath. All you can think of is how you can get out. I constantly made excuses for his behavior, pretending that certain things were completely normal. Little did I know that this was his insecurities being transferred to me. Soon these insecurities came out when he was drunk and would verbally abuse me in any way he could think of and blame me for everything other than the reason he was born. Again, I excused it under the premise that he was drunk and didn't mean it. These behaviors started to escalate the more I tried to pull away. I tried to leave many times but he would become crazy. There are some things I chose not to say because of how painful it is to discuss. The one day I said enough was when he threatened my life. It wasn't an easy process to get him out of my life; in fact, it took months of harassment and living in fear. Regardless of the fear, I knew I had made the right decision to leave. I thought that the abuse was over, but little did I know that even after he was gone, I would suffer mentally, all of which I kept to myself. I just put on a smile and took every day as if this had all never happened to me. Trying to be in new relationships and chasing my dreams seemed impossible inside, but on the outside, it was if I was just like any other teen.

From here it seemed that a dark cloud followed me everywhere I went. A year later, I experienced my first taste of death, and little did I know that this was the first of many to come. I lost both my grandfathers a year apart from each other. I never truly confronted the grief and pain this caused me. As a matter of fact, I ignored any sense of pain. When I thought that it was all over and I could breathe again, I got a phone call from my dad. He said my mom had ovarian cancer. I collapsed into the arms of my boyfriend, who is now my husband. For once in my life, it's as if all the pain I had been carrying for years washed over me like a tidal wave, only this time, it felt endless. Living with a sick parent is one of the hardest things I have ever had to do. Watching a parent suffer every day for almost five years is one of the worst things the soul has to bear. The years my mother battled cancer were the most heartbreaking, numbing, and loneliest days I have experienced. It was almost as if I was walking through a cloud of smoke and not being able to see any light at the end of the tunnel. Just clouds. My university graduation was bittersweet. Near the end of my mom's battle with cancer, she garnered the strength to come to my graduation. Watching her do this for me made me forget about everything and only see love in its purest form. The day before she died she told me she loved me. She sounded like she was more alive than any other day.

The emotional struggle began…

From the day she died up until two years later, life was a haze. In that time, I also lost my grandmother. No feeling, just moving through the motions. I felt I should go back to work because I was expected to just snap out of grief. Employment almost seemed impossible as I went through jobs that my mental state just could not handle. This broke me down further, feeling like I couldn't do anything wholeheartedly because let's face it; I had so much unresolved pain. Every new pain became worse than the last because I didn't deal with it. I thought the pain would just disappear if I put my best foot forward. Year three was pure anger. Almost everything had me feeling enraged. Year four I became engaged to the love of my life who has stood by me through everything. As happy as I was, everything now became bittersweet because I knew she wouldn't be here to celebrate, to coach me, to be my friend, to be the voice giving me advice, to hug me, to kiss me, to give me her blessings, to be the one person in my corner. I realized that my biggest fan was really gone. Life as I knew it became bittersweet. I just couldn't seem to be completely happy. There was always a "but." I realized that something within me had to change. I had to find happiness again. But what is happiness? After being in a whirlwind of trauma since the age of fifteen, I had no clue how to be joyful because I had been living in a state of unhappiness for so long, pretending to be okay. I was exhausted. Tired of being okay and strong for everyone but myself. Tired of doing what was expected, what the norm was. I woke up and realized that the "norm" was clearly not my life and I needed to do what was best for me…and be okay with it, regardless of what the world thought. My struggle was my own and I needed to own it, take care of it, and heal it. But still, I had no clue how to. I had seen glimpses of what should be done to heal, but it's as if pain covered it all and I couldn't focus. It felt like there was so much noise and confusion that I had no clue where to start. Nearing year five of my mother's passing, I married my loving husband. When we returned from our destination wedding, it was as if the answers came to me.

The time finally came…

I knew the time to change had come. I went on a leave of absence from work and took time to realize that I was broken and that was okay. I started to look within myself for answers. I started to address the issues, the pain, the sadness, the hurt, the anger. I have begun to tell my story and be okay with being vulnerable. I have let many individuals who have been through similar struggles coach me and guide me to becoming the best person that I can be. I decided that I needed to see a counselor. In fact, I saw two. One to help me with grief and the other helped me with coping and changing my thoughts. I have let out all that has been trapped inside for so long. Keeping calm through this new chapter in my life is only half the battle. It is realizing when it is brewing and being able to recognize it, and reach out and connect to those who are around us, is where I have found my inner power and strength. I am now connected to a life coach to help me stay on track to living the life I want. I have reconnected with who I really am. I am a person that loves to be creative. I have reconnected with writing, art, and music. I have now made it my mission to find my happy place every day. However, my story is not done. I am still a work in progress, but have finally been able to close a chapter of pain and move to a mindset of carving my path to happiness by any means necessary.

Janine Berridge Paul's life path has truly opened her eyes and has shown her that the road to happiness and empowerment is in one's hands. Her experiences have allowed Janine to value her quiet time where she enjoys reflecting on life, love, creativity, and the beauty of imagination. She values giving back to the community through her work with youth and those involved in the justice system. Janine hopes to take her passions one step further by starting her own business and writing her own book. She is also a devoted wife and comes from a Caribbean family that is rich in culture.

Email: Berridge.janine@gmail.com

Linkedin - Janine Berridge

Empower Boost

How Reiki Can Help You Heal
by Andrea Lavallee

Reiki is a well-known alternative way to make the body feel better and is also a great pain reliever. How does it work you ask? I will tell you. When you are receiving Reiki from a Reiki practitioner, they have been attuned by their Reiki Master and have been taught symbols to help bring in Reiki energy that helps to align the energy, relax the body and the mind, and is therefore able to raise your vibration and heal the body. It is when your body is at a higher vibration that healing and pain relief can occur. Typically, Reiki is done in silence and works with your energy center or Charkas. During a session, the energy knows where it needs to go to aid in healing.

Some of the benefits of being in a high vibrational state:

- You feel energized and radiant.
- You feel supported, safe, and secure.
- You become empowered.
- You experience increased clarity and awareness.
- You feel alive and free.
- You effortlessly achieve more balance in life.
- You take on a youthful glow and a childlike exuberance.
- Your health naturally improves.

- You are confident and enthusiastic.
- You experience synchronicity consistently.
- You get in the flow and life becomes easy.
- You consistently think and feel empowering emotions.

Just like Reiki is able to raise your vibration, invite healing, and relieve pain, there are many other means that can raise your vibration and invite healing, such as thinking positive thoughts, eating healthier, affirmations, visualization, having a positive mindset, and really feeling good about yourself. The list can go on and on.

Interactive Reiki is combining Reiki with positive thoughts, affirmations, and Empowerment coaching during a Reiki session. The client and Reiki practitioner discuss goals or intentions prior to the start of the session. During the Reiki session, the client is given positive thoughts in relation to their goals or intentions to repeat silently to themselves which raises their vibration. In essence, while the client is silently repeating their phrase or words, the Reiki practitioner is working in tandem with the Reiki energy. This raises the vibration to a whole new level which brings on a greater healing process.

Here is how it works. A client comes in and requests, for example, that they would like to lose weight. Prior to the session, they would receive coaching on what the "real" issue is related to unsuccessful weight loss in the past. Once they are on the massage table for Reiki, I would use my intuition and give key phrases that will help them gain some insight and clarity. As I go through each charka area, I would have them repeat several different phases such as "I am in complete control of my cravings." If I am working over the heart charka for example, I may have my client say, "I love myself and my choices." Over the solar plexus, I may have them say the word "Release." You can really feel the shift in energy more so with Interactive Reiki, compared to a non-interactive Reiki session. Once the vibration is high on both ends, then the energy can bring on the healing, relief pain, give insight and clarity. For the most part, the session is only half interactive and the other half is usually done in silence. It all depends on the client and their goals.

This process works great for pain, infertility, and all other mind-body matters.

Andrea Lavallee is an Empowerment Awareness Consultant and Life Coach. She is the founder of The Empowerment Coaching Group, and the host of the International radio show, The Life Coach Radio Show. Andrea is available for live speaking opportunities, in person workshops, and one-on-one coaching.

https://www.facebook.com/empowermentcoachingbyandrea

Chapter 26

How to Feel Free and Alive...
by Lisa Berry

Clearly this was a huge mistake!

I was actually an adult trapped in a child's body and it pained me to have to go through years of torture and punishment to finally get into that adult body that would allow me to express my own choice.

It's funny how society gives privilege in exchange for "doing time," or as we are more commonly familiar with, "years of living" on the planet, and not because of one's conscious awareness.

This was my mindset growing up. Having lived now in my adult body for quite some time, I do recognize the value and reasons for having to go through the growing up and maturing process but none the less as a child I truly couldn't wait to be a real woman, an adult, my entire life! Ohh what freedom I would have!

Me living my freedom doesn't come without its judgments or its curiosity from others, but it does deliver me my true happiness.

Barefoot, self-employed, creator, and cat mom, I truly love my life!

As a child, the "why" question wasn't as important to me as the "now what" question. The ability to respond was power to me. I wanted to choose how I would respond because I could witness how others reacted and then could decide if that outcome looked like I'd enjoy it or not.

It was great having an older sister because she'd always go first. Big things, little things, she was my view into a possible future. My sister ended up being my very first mentor and coach.

My parents, who I strongly believe I personally selected before being born, offered me endless opportunities to grow. Never a dull moment and never without love, guidance, and an open book of possibilities. My mom endured a very painful life, filled with not just daily suffering but every minute she lived was chosen from a place of how to be the most comfortable she could be with the conditions and illnesses she had. My dad with his commitment and positive attitude supported by an unwavering faith of love was always brainstorming with us all the possibilities that our family could choose to be healthy, abundant, and happy.

My two biggest challenges as a child were firstly that I expressed my ownership of my life exuberantly; however I lacked the maturity to do so in a way that adults felt comfortable allowing. The statement that I heard the most was probably "I'm the mom, you're the child."

The other challenge was that I forgave instantly, held no grudges, and believed guilt was useless. This made it very difficult for me to understand why others were unhappy or walked through life holding onto pain. It hurt me to see others not forgive, not move forward, and not exercise their right to make the choice of happiness for themselves.

When I say that I found guilt to be useless, it's not to say I wasn't an extremely compassionate child, it's that I quickly realized and acknowledged my wrongdoing and immediately offered a heartfelt apology. My mom was the one to teach me the lesson that others, including herself, couldn't move on that quickly and needed more…perhaps more time, perhaps more comfort from the person who did wrong, or maybe just more belief that people can be sorry and loving. I learned the lesson of "self-protection" from her. I realized I needed to self-protect but more than that, I learned that how others treated me was because of how they were feeling and it wasn't really about me. This was gold!

I started understanding this lesson in the reverse as well. How I treated people was about ME and not much about them. Again, another power tool. I gathered these power nuggets all throughout my childhood years and was excited to be given that title, that privilege, that the title "Adult" brings.

I moved out as soon as I could and my chosen career at the time was a counselor at a weight loss clinic. Growing up with a very ill mother gave me a solid background in anatomy and how the body works. It was fun and fulfilling for me to be able to support women through their weight challenges. Basically, we were taught how to micro manage the body's responses to each menu and regime these ladies desperately tried. The science of weight loss is what led me to nutrition and soon I found out that holistic nutrition existed. This was the jack pot of schools for me. Though I was extremely academic and found school rather easy, I struggled with the schedule structure, or how I refer to it as confinement! I'm sure my parents thought I was an activist for human rights as I was stubborn and took committed action on doing what I wanted to because it felt right to me. That of course included me feeling like the act of going to school was a sentence. I hated wearing anything on my feet and in Canada not only is it necessary at times, it's simply the law for public places and etiquette in regards to social matters. The powerful distraction of being uncomfortable though made me sick. I couldn't think, my attitude declined, and eventually I'd feel ill, get a headache, and truly become physically sick.

One can easily see how it was a must that I do only what I loved, to be comfortable in order to be productive. It in fact became what I represented! Choice and decision making showed up to me everywhere: in advertisements, in conversations, in friendships, and in my coaching career. The question "Is this what you want to do?" started developing layers as if it was a course. I started cultivating this question and creating my entire life and career around it. Stuck, stagnant, need a shift? This is my power question I ask to all.

When we are stuck, stagnant, or we need a shift, it's a form of suffering to me. My mom suffered every day of her life that I witnessed and yet she continually and bravely would show me how she explored possibilities, choices, and exercised her personal power to make the best of her time. We didn't call it meditation then, but she performed all kinds of it such as knitting or listening to classical or Scottish music. She mindfully detached herself from the pain with carefully selected movies as to either enhance or dissolve an emotion. My mom would be clear and concise when asking for what she needed whether it was quiet or communication.

Family pets were an absolute joy and responsibility. My mom with her very animated face would speak for our cats, dogs, and guinea pigs… she gave them a voice and a deep respect for animals was instilled in me. Animals in the house were kind of tricky though as dad was extremely allergic and yet with his desire for his family and his wife to be happy, he chose to put his own breathing needs aside. I in fact never knew that he was allergic to our animals and thought that dads just blew their noses a lot. A very selfless man he was, and is, and taught me that we also have the power to make decisions to sacrifice for other's wellbeing though our own may be hindered.

Every night I go to bed with gratitude and every day I wake up with excitement for all the choices I get to make. Even when I do a life review and know that many of my choices brought me to results I didn't originally want, I'm still grateful and happy that it was me who decided to try that experience. Possibilities exist – it's my responsibility to seek them out. Choices are mine to make and it's me who gets to make them. Responses, my responses come from me and I get to act them out. The best part is I can adjust, shift, or change my responses when I chose. For me, life isn't about going against the grain, proving anyone wrong, or being different. It's about alignment with my heart and making sure I'm living the life I want. My personal power comes from respecting and loving myself and having gratitude and joy for MY life no matter what age I am.

Lisa Berry is an expert in breathing life into the dreams of those wanting to live vibrantly, energetically, happy, and fulfilled while standing confidently and strongly rooted in their personal power. She has turned up the natural light of hundreds of clients by helping them move from a place of trapped, scarred, or numb to a place of possibilities, choices, and feeling empowered to respond after listening to the hearts. Lisa fulfills her commitment as a Transitional Coach and Registered Holistic Nutritionist as she recognizes her mission to find, help, and connect with those who need and want to shine.

lisa@datingyourdiet.ca

1 (647) 449-4569

Empower Boost

Just When You Think All the Cards Are Dealt...
by Lori Canlas - De Pala M.S.W., R.S.W.

Sometimes it helps to be pushed into a corner, knowing the only way out of a nerve-wracking situation is to confront your fear head on. It is ludicrous to think that everybody who wants to confront his or her fear wakes up in the morning saying, "I'm ready! Bring on the fear!" Yes, it's not that simple. Most of us are in limbo, and we deliberate what may be the best move to a point where we run out of options. You are not alone in your experience.

When Archimedes, an ancient Greek Mathematician, had coined the term "Eureka," he had excitedly stumbled upon a unique discovery. What do I do to unravel being nervous and scared about unfolding the path less taken? Most of us are so used to being comfortably nestled in what is known and the routine of life. However, it doesn't allow you to grasp your dreams.

Risk taking will take you to knowing that the next moment may be your last breath, and by acknowledging this possibility, you can always live on the verge of discovery. You can be in awe, knowing that you can make a global impact on other people's lives. You are made to be great despite stumbling upon misfortunes. However, misfortunes fertilize the blossoming of your dreams. We are living in an age where we have a mightier ability to create a ripple effect. We are interconnected in this web of life. I would like to encourage you that your life matters even if you've been set back with failures. You can be propelled into greatness in a moment's time. Breathe it and live it.

Lori Canlas-De Pala is a Life Coach, a Registered Social Worker, has a Master's degree in Social Work, and is the founder of Bridging Dialogue Consulting. Lori's philosophy is "We cannot function to our fullest capacity until we have cared for ourselves. Caring for oneself allows us to fully care for others."

www.bridgingdialogueconsulting.ca

Chapter 27

Regina's Journey
by Regina Neal

As a little girl, I enjoyed playing make-believe and dreamed of how my life would be when I was an adult. Pretending made me happy. I fancied getting married, being a teacher, having four children (two of each), and living happily-ever-after. In reality, I did not become a teacher because I left school before I finished, married at age 17½, had two daughters, and was a single mom at age twenty-three. How could this happen? How could my dreams of a life full of happiness and hope become a life of unhappiness? I felt hopeless, confused, frustrated, alone, and desperate. What went wrong? Can you relate to any of this? Has something similar happened to you?

In my search for answers, I looked back on my childhood. Now, my memory is not perfect, but it seemed to me that we lacked for nothing. We had a home, food, and clothing. In our community of 500, few families had nicer homes, nicer clothes, and more to eat. Those families with fewer kids were a tad better off. I was the eldest of seven children in our family – less food to go around. It was not obvious to me that we were poor. I was ten years old before we had a TV, but we were the only ones in our little group who had one.

My life did not feel poor. In my eyes, we had everything: space to play, trees to climb, berries to pick, brooks to fish, an ocean to swim in, clothes to wear, and food to eat. It was a wonderland from a kid's viewpoint. I do not ever recall being "bored," not even on rainy days. Occasionally, food was a little short, but we did not go hungry. There was always a piece of homemade bread with butter and molasses or jam. When at my friend's home, her mom would give me bread with molasses or jam. At home, my Mom did the same for my friend. Everyone looked out for one another. Yes, I received the occasional spanking, but I deserved it every time – well…maybe – except for a couple of times.

The first time I sensed a lack of confidence I was about eight. My grandparents' property was in front of ours, and they had a large field. One day they had visitors who had children. All the neighborhood kids were there playing games. My parents said we could join them, but first, we needed to be cleaned up and change into better clothing.

My brother (age six), sister (age four), and I went to our grandparents where we stood on the sideline watching the other children play. We smiled and watched as they played and had fun. We waited to be asked to join in. Several times, I tried to ask, "Can we play, too?" The words stuck like a lump in my throat. A few times my brother or sister prompted me to ask, but I did not. I could not get the words out. We spent the whole time standing there, watching and waiting for an invitation from the other children. No one said, "Want to play?" On the way back home, I felt bad because I had let my brother and sister down.

My parents, who could see the activities in the yard next door, said, "I thought you went over to play." I said, "We did." Mom said, "Then, why didn't you play?" "I don't know," I said, looking down at the floor.

How could I tell my parents I was afraid to ask? How could I tell them that the other children did not invite us to play? They did not like us. Feeling ashamed, I went to my bedroom to play alone.

I began seventh grade at age twelve, which until 1967 was high school in Newfoundland. We traveled forty-five minutes to school by bus to Stephenville (pop. 18,000). The first school day was exciting for my friends and me, but that quickly changed. My self-confidence took a beating that year. I understood for the first time the meaning of being rich. I did not want to be like them nor waste my time trying to befriend their kind. The behavior of the rich kids was terrible. They were snobs, acted superior to us, and took every opportunity to show it. Because they were better dressed, they teased us about our clothing. The boys were only interested in the pretty rich girls and those girls were mean. I quickly made the assumption that Rich = Snobby and Pretty Girls = Mean. That was how I felt, sad but true. It wouldn't be until I was thirty before another experience caused me to change my beliefs about pretty girls/women and rich people.

All through high school, I allowed other people's opinion of me to determine how I felt about myself. High school was no longer exciting for me. I became quiet and reserved. I hated reading aloud in school or answering questions, even when I had the correct answer. I was afraid to appear too smarter and stumbled over my words. I blushed, which told everyone I was embarrassed, and that left me open to teasing. I detested being shy and having attention drawn to me. Shyness may be cute at age two but not as a teen or adult. Shyness and insecurity affected all areas of my life. My confidence faded. My dream of pursuing a teaching career was dashed. Obviously, I was not good enough. I developed an Inadequate Self-Image (ISI) and lost hope. I saw myself as unworthy, unable to fulfill my dreams, and have a happier life.

At age sixteen, I started dating my future husband; he was twenty-seven. We were engaged on my seventeenth birthday. I had no interest in finishing school, so we planned our wedding for that summer. Two months before my wedding, I had second thoughts about leaving school early, and wanted to postpone the marriage until I finished high school and graduated with my friends. My fiancé would not hear of it. He said, "If you love me, you marry me now. It is now or not at all." This should have been a clue to me, but I was afraid of losing him. We were married as planned. I became a new mom at age eighteen and was twenty when my second daughter was born.

My husband turned out to be unreliable and a poor provider for our family. I had to go to work to help support us despite our plan for me to stay home until our children were in school full-time. By the age of twenty-three, I was unhappy and exhausted from fighting with my husband. I packed up, took my daughters, who were five and three years old, and left our home.

My new situation was frightening to me. I lacked the courage to go after what I wanted and missed out on many opportunities to enjoy life. I felt alone and desperate from doing everything by myself. I hoped for a better life without knowing how to get it. I was on the outside looking in on a life I did not understand. No one to rely on. No one to help me.

On many occasions, I was forced to step out of my comfort zone for the sake of my daughters. My mom often said, "Forced put is no man's choice." We make hard decisions at tough times in our lives; sometimes, those decisions turn out to be the best choices after all. In hindsight, my tough decisions were blessings. I did not permit myself the luxury of wallowing in self-pity. For the sake of my daughters, I keep doing my best, like it or not.

After years of searching to find my way and enduring another broken heart, I moved to Toronto in 1981 with my daughters and stayed with my sister. Living in a small town back home, I would always say "hello" to anyone I met on the street. It was the polite thing to do. In Toronto, I was overwhelmed and found the city unwelcoming. It was hard for me to make friends. Some people misinterpreted my natural reserve to mean I wanted to be left alone. Being shy and insecure resulted in me feeling very alone and foregoing on more opportunities.

In 1985, came the next improvement point in my life. I joined a cosmetics franchise, a home-show company that required me to stand in front of a group of ladies to demo the products. I was so nervous during my first presentation; I thought I was going to die. Guess what? I survived, started gaining confidence, and getting good at doing demos. It was a few years later when it struck me that I was actually living my childhood dream of being a teacher. Helping others look and feel their best improved their confidence. It was rewarding for me to see the transformation in my customers, which in turn, produced a jolt of confidence in me. I loved my work.

The next phase of my life occurred when I heard an incredible motivational speaker at a conference. I was so impressed with his philosophy and beliefs that I purchased one of his best-selling books. My mind flew open by the lessons he taught. There was hope for me! I was not doomed to failure and unhappiness all my life. As I read, scenes from my life flashed through my head telling me where I went wrong, what I should have done, and what I should have avoided. The most important lesson: my mind can only carry one thought at a time, that being a positive thought or a negative thought. Above all, I learned that I possessed the power to control the thoughts in my mind. I was hooked on new potentials I did not know existed. There was no turning back. My pursuit of personal development had begun. In the beginning, it took me months to read a book, so I turned my car into a University-On-Wheels and listened to cassette tapes. At home, it was CDs, VHS tapes, and DVDs. Although slow at first, soon my reading speed improved. I was on my way to a better life.

I discovered that if I wanted something bad enough, I could find a way. I was hungry and on a mission to improve my life. In order to help others, I had to help myself first me. I was excited about the possibilities. One quote I had read really stuck with me: *"You can have everything in life you want if you help enough other people get what they want."* - Zig Ziglar. Yup! That's me. I am in.

In 1985, I married for a second time hoping this marriage would be more successful than the first. This relationship was a blended family with its own dynamics. With much interference from outside sources and difficulties from within, the marriage ended in 1992. With two failed marriages behind me, my heart was broken and my self-esteem took another troubling downturn. Again, I had to pick myself up and dust myself off to keep going. The only person I could depend on was me. My daughters, in their own special ways, encouraged me. Little by little my thoughts and attitude changed. With small adjustments, patience, determination, and questioning my beliefs, I discovered my truth. Hope filled my heart.

Although I have struggled the majority of my life and made many mistakes, most of my growth came from the worse trials and lessons I learned. Now, when difficulties come, I say, "Here I grow again." Then I prepare myself. Today, I am victorious, in a twenty-four-year relationship, and enjoying my life more fully. Yes, there are still ups and downs, but I can handle them much better now. I am in control of my destiny, and it's a powerful feeling. I enjoy coaching others toward feeling powerful.

As long as I can remember, I have seen people struggle just like I did, pulled in opposite directions by conflicting beliefs and opinions imposed on them, caught up in a tangle of uncertainty and sorrow. We look for approval from others and don't trust our own judgment. We strive to be like our friends and neighbors, and keep up with what society says we should have or do. In the process, we lose ourselves and our dreams trying to keep up with the Jones' family. Even the Jones cannot keep up with the Jones. That is not our purpose. Our goal is to live our dreams, which come from within us. We would not be given such dreams that we could not make come true. It is in our DNA to survive and thrive.

We are responsible for being our best by utilizing the tools and talents we have at that moment. As we learn and grow, we develop and prosper. With the new skills, we will do better, achieve more, and fill our minds with the right stuff.

Live your passion. Don't know what you are passionate about? Take a long look at your childhood. The clues are there. What did you love to do most of the time? What did you see yourself doing as an adult? Are you doing it? Maybe revisit what you had loved doing as a child and incorporate it into your career. It will make your heart sing. It is a terrible thing to earn a living working at a job you dislike. If you cannot change careers, at least do what you love as a hobby. It will balance out your workday. You were created for greatness.

"We were designed for accomplishment, engineered for success and endowed with the seeds of greatness." - Zig Ziglar

Love yourself. You deserve it! You owe it to yourself. Love with all your heart. Love is magical. No matter how much love you give away, there is always more love to give. The more you love, the more love you receive in return.

Strive to be as happy as possible no matter what the situation may be. Ask for forgiveness, if you have hurt someone. It does not matter who was right or who was wrong – clear the air. Forgive those who hurt you. If you do not forgive, you are allowing them to hurt you over, and over, and over again – you deserve much better than that.

For too long, I have allowed other people's opinion of me (real or imagined) to determine my decisions whether I followed my dreams or not. This held me back from fulfilling my life's purpose – being the best that I could be with whatever circumstances I was dealing with at that particular moment. Most of the time, the drama was in my mind and not factual.

Remember: Nothing means nothing until you attach a meaning to it and your mind can only carry one thought at a time. Will that thought be positive or negative? Which thought do you want to occupy the prime real estate of your mind?

Do you want to reclaim control of your life, but don't know where to start or don't see a way? Then meet Regina Neal, a personal development expert who specializes in attitude adjustments, taking you from "Victim to Victor!" Transform your life with this author, speaker, and host of talk radio "You Matter!" Her mission is to boost confidence and courage for anyone facing stress, insecurity, and overwhelm using simple steps and strategies. Regina provides a refreshing perspective and break from textbook psychology. She proudly claims, "I trained at the University of Hard Knocks and returned occasionally for refresher courses."

www.youniquely.biz

reginaneal@gmail.com

Empower Boost

Is Happiness a Myth?
by Andrea Lavallee

When a well-known Hollywood actor/comedian had passed away, I recall millions of people asking, "Why?" "He seemed to have it all." It really made me wonder if happiness is a myth. As someone who has been "searching for happiness" for as long as I can remember, I have wondered for years about that question. I was constantly asking myself, "Why can't I be happy? When will I be happy?" I thought all I need to do was get married, have children, or even just have lots of money. I have noticed that there is always something missing. I've learned that it's good to have the proper tools in place to help you get through your difficult times when they hit.

I strongly believe that we are all here on earth to learn and to grow, and we need to realize that in order for that to happen, we need to have challenging times, trials, difficulties, and pain – for two reasons: first, so that we can appreciate the better times even more, and secondly, for growth. So, there will be good times and bad times. Like seasons, we need only to anticipate and prepare for them. One of my virtual mentor, J.R., said, "Don't wish it was easier wish you were better. Don't wish for less problems wish for more skills. Don't wish for less challenge wish for more wisdom." How true is that for growth!?

So trials make us grow and learn, and at the end of them, we are able to appreciate the better times even more. My suggestion: anticipate and appreciate difficulties. It will make them a little easier to get through; also, make wise choices as the consequences to our actions are not a choice. As well, have some tools in your tool box for when they do come around. For myself, I like to tap (also known as EFT) away my challenges or write in my gratitude journal, and when they get too much to bear and hopelessness sets in, I pray. I mean I really pray. The kind where you get down on your knees and have an outpouring of your heart with a feeling of gratitude behind it. That really makes the burdens feel lighter every time.

I have come to realize that happiness was always within my grasp all along. Yup, I realized that it was up to me. It turned out that only I could make myself happy and that happiness is a choice. Once I figured that out, I started smiling more and was able to freely share more of myself with others who needed my help because nothing makes me happier than helping others to be happy.

Andrea Lavallee is an Empowerment Awareness Consultant and Life Coach. She is the founder of The Empowerment Coaching Group, and the host of the International radio show, The Life Coach Radio Show. Andrea is available for live speaking opportunities, in person workshops, and one-on-one coaching.

https://www.facebook.com/empowermentcoachingbyandrea

Chapter 28

The Little Engine That Can
by Tina Gaisin

I am a four-time cancer survivor and a single mom of four kids! The reason I tell you this is not so you will feel sorry for me, but that if someone comes into your life that needs to hear my story, you can share it and they can contact me. It is my passion to help others going through cancer, or families, to get the emotional and spiritual help they need. People have helped me and I want to assist others.

Today I reflect on the child that I was growing up and the path that I have followed. I was a strong soul with a good heart and today I am still that strong woman. I always knew that I had a higher purpose and that I wanted to help others shine. As a child, I always befriended the new student in our class. You know them – they're the ones who are awkward and shy. Today I still do the same thing.

Over the decades I have had the opportunity to save the lives of others, whether it was a drowning child, a car accident, a choking man, a motorcyclist, or a person running a marathon. If I had to ask myself why, again I feel there is something within myself that says, "Go and be there. You will be able to help others to live."

Today as I reflect on my life, I was abused while growing up and I had to grow up fast. I made excuses for other's behaviors, yet I took the flack and did not speak up. I became the victim. After much soul searching and many mentors and coaches over the years (some big names), I finally get that I am a strong empowered person.

Think about this – what if I did not have challenges in my early life? How would my life today be different? I know that each challenge was not an uphill climb but the journey to lead me to goodness and happiness. The funny thing is, as life gets great, major obstacles come into my way! I totally believe it is how I deal with each occurrence. Even the people that come into my life, I always believe in everyone's good soul until they prove me wrong. I have been stuck with several bad influences and yet I have learned something from each and every one. The only thing I would do, if I could go back in time, is to not be stuck with the wrong person because I somehow needed them in my life at that time.

Lately, as I talk to my children and see their struggles, I want to impart the wisdom I have on them. I have to hold back, because I am just "MOM" and I don't know anything. I can tell them stories but I have to let them make their own choices and decisions.

On my life's journey, I have encountered great leaders who have shaped me. Each of their teachings helped me and although sometimes it did not feel as if I took them to heart at that time, in my time I did, and I am appreciative of them in my life.

The road to health and healing is not always an easy one, but I have three things that are extremely important to me and became my mission in life. They are HaShem (G-d), healing the world back to health, and starting with me. Every change that comes cannot be from others but it starts from me.

When I was going through my third bout of cancer, I wanted to sing and dance because I could barely talk for six months. It was my holiday called Purim and I was dancing. A friend said to me, "Why do you have such a great attitude?" I asked her, "Why?" She said, "You are close to dying! You shouldn't be acting that way!" She was always so negative and it made it difficult to be with her. Your attitude or the ways you deal with life's lessons are the way you will get through them.

I have successful businesses, both in the past and currently, that I started! The most important act I do is give back to those that need it most and not judge. Each time you give, you will get back tenfold. People will have hard times and there will always be people that struggle with what they have received in life. I like to think that by helping them be successful, they too will "pay it forward" and help others as well. For example, when going through one of my bouts of cancer and all that it entailed, I decided I needed peer support for myself and for my kids. I was able to do cathartic art that I loved and felt passionate about. The lady teaching donated her time to help people who were going through treatment. I helped the art teacher make peace with her mother who died of cancer.

Having been a teenager who thought that life was over, and making a conscious decision that life was what I made it, I had/have the power to make my way as a strong determined woman who loves getting out of bed in the morning whether the sun shines or not. I feel that each of us has a mission in life and a song that resonates within us. I am like the little train engine that could – not only do I think I can, but I knew I could. My song is *"I will Survive!"* by Gloria Gaynor and *"Margaritaville"* by Jimmy Buffett. Another well-known American singer and actress' music makes me happy too. Whenever I need to have a little uplift I play my favorite songs, or sing them! I can drown out the negative lyrics of songs that sometimes tell me I am not worthy. Playing the music loud and singing only leaves happiness.

Abused as a child, sexually abused as a teenager, verbally abused throughout my life, married the wrong husband – I should have been so much more bitter. But I'm not, although I had to work through what I call the muck to get to the other side, and I am. I am a life, business, and communication coach. I am a Distinguished Toastmaster (DTM) and a BT, and I have been coached, mentored, and had my "tush kicked" by many notable people. When I think of life's "aha" moments, the greatest teachings have come from my kids, whether they are happy or sad, love me, or hate me. I have learned a lot from them and I love them very much. When children are from a broken marriage, I see a lot of them suffering and having a hard time with the right partner for them. My millennial children constantly get me thinking about right and wrong and how I could have done better for them. When they came into this world, they did not have a manual attached. I did not have a manual for when my marriage ended and the years it would take to get divorced. I made mistakes and was not perfect. Saying that and realizing that has been a major breakthrough. I am MOM and I am supposed to be perfect. In business I am not perfect; then why as a mom am I not perfect? Who says moms have to be perfect? I can only say that each of my four children were planned, wanted, and loved – then and now. I did and do my best as a mom. I only hope that being a "Bubie" will be easier when the time comes and that I can do fun things with the grandkids, and that my children and my stepchildren appreciate that.

I have a special honey in my life (calling him a boyfriend is too strange – we are way too old for that!). He and I met several times randomly while we were both married. I believe that I met and re-met my special someone after going after the wrong ones. I believe I cannot ever look back and think, "What did I do wrong? Why did I go with that person? Why was I friends with that one?" Rather I thank them and look forward to the great people and challenges that will come my way. I have been on television, radio, and have won The Woman Entrepreneur of the Year Award. I am an advisor with a great marketing association and life is wonderful. I am making it great. I'm excited about the opportunity to be part of this compilation with other amazing people who are making empowerment part of their lives.

I am having a great ride and the future is very exciting. Live life as if it was your last moment, and love the people around you like it is the last time you will see them.

As a four-time cancer survivor and a single mom with four kids, Tina Gaisin has a passion for life. She is a sailor, a DTM (Distinguished Toastmaster award) and loves to help others! She is a Business Coach, Communication Coach, and a Life Coach with over several decades' worth of certifications! She is a keynote speaker and helps you to become one as well! Tina is a thirty-six year Volunteer with the Red Cross and has helped many businesses to get more noticed, higher sales, and has even won several awards in business! She is also an Advisor of CAMP (Canadian Association of Marketing Professionals).

tinagaisin@yahoo.ca

Section Two:

Stories of Being Empowered by an Individual or Community

I've come to believe that each of us has a personal calling that's as unique as a fingerprint – and that the best way to succeed is to discover what you love and then find a way to offer it to others in the form of service, working hard, and also allowing the energy of the universe to lead you. — Oprah Winfrey

Imagine being inspired by a loving parent, to have love and adoration for the commitment and sacrifice they have made for you and the lessons you have learned about life because of their examples. You may not have appreciated them then, but you do now and you are humbled to share their legacy, and to write about it, and promote it to the world so that others can benefit from their efforts.

Envision being motivated by gaining knowledge, or the love for music, or allowing social media to change your life by bringing empowerment right to your living room, being a survivor because of the community you belong to, or maybe your community opened your eyes and encouraged you to become something better.

These are the type of stories that you are about to read. Meet the people who have been empowered by others, and have gained strength due to someone else's example and hard work.

You might want to ask yourself after reading these stores, "What am I doing to help empower someone else's world?" or "How can my gifts and talents help another to live a more fulfilled life?" You never know who could be inspired by you, so why not live your empowered life by being an example of virtue and positivity.

Andrea Lavallee

Empowerment Awareness Life Coach, Author, Reiki Master

Chapter 29

Embracing Life's Lessons: 10 Tips to Live a More Empowered Life. Part 1

by Andrea Lavallee

1) **Life can be full of challenges, which will encourage you to GROW.**

   I usually hate being challenged, but whenever I look back at one, I always think, "That situation really worked out well for me. If it hadn't happened, I would not have reached my new goal, which is better than my old goal." After being challenged a few times, I realized that whenever a new situation popped up, it was because I needed to learn something which, if I chose wisely, made me a better and stronger person.

When my finances were upside-down because I was unemployed while trying to build the business of my dreams, I was constantly being tested financially. I didn't know how I was going to pay some of my bills. I was tapping into whatever I could until there was nothing left to turn to. And that was painful; I wanted to cry all the time because I felt like such a failure. But I knew that I could not give up; I needed to keep going no matter what. I knew that it would not kill me, and in time I figured out that I just needed to take it one day at a time. In the end, I learned that I needed to keep better track of my finances and that I needed to learn how to ask for help. I became more humble and a better money manager. And boy, did I grow! I became stronger emotionally because I had no choice than to get out there and build my business. Although at times that was very difficult, it was all worth it.

What challenges did or do you have in your life that has or is encouraging you to grow? Please make a note on a separate piece of paper.

2) **Being truly grateful is the key to HAPPINESS.**

   To be truly grateful can be difficult when you're in a situation that you are not happy with. But to be honest, that is just Law of Attraction 101! If you want to get to a better situation, you have to be grateful for what you have now; the more you appreciate what you have at this moment, the more you will get what you desire in the future. You always attract to yourself the things that you are focusing on. If you are in a state of ungratefulness, then your focus will be skewed and you will attract more of what you do not want! Stay positive!

   Once I was able to wrap my head around that concept, I worked really hard at being grateful for all of the little things in my life, right down to the bed that I slept in. Results came quickly, and I realized that I was starting to attract the things that made my life easier.

   I can remember how I felt as I was going through my healing phase when, leaving my last job turned out to be a very difficult and trying situation for me. I had to be grateful to the people that had mistreated me (I also had to forgive them) and grateful that I now was able to do what I loved and to spend more time with my son. It was a very powerful experience. So now when things get challenging in life or with building my business, I think of the gratefulness that I have for my employer who had made it all possible.

   What are some things in your life that you are truly grateful for? Please make a note on a separate piece of paper.

3) **You cannot change your PURPOSE, but you can start LIVING it.**

   No matter how much you try to get away from your purpose, somehow it will always keep finding you.

   I always knew I wanted to work with energy, as I was continually close to the Spirit. But in all honesty, I had been hiding it and was ashamed of it. However, the more I tried to find something else to do and get passionate about, the dissatisfied I became. I felt unfulfilled. Once I stopped hiding it and started letting my skills be known, then I started really living, being my true self, and starting to grow into the person I was meant to become.

   What is your true purpose? If you don't know it by now, what are some things that bring you joy, make you feel empowered, and make you feel fulfilled – there needs to be an element of helping others or serving in some way as that's what it's about – Learning, Growing and Serving. Please make a note on a separate piece of paper.

4) **Sometimes you need to EXPERIENCE what you *don't* want to, if you really need to know what you *do* want.**

   As much as you don't like something, always be grateful for it, because its purpose may be to teach you what you do not want for yourself. It's nice to know what you do want, but if you don't also experience a little of what you don't want, then you will never appreciate what you do want when you get it. You may just take it for granted, so be grateful for everything.

   This was huge for me because all I could think about was how perfect things would be once I got what I wanted. My focus was so set on the good times I would have in the future, that it made every little crisis get blown way out of proportion. But once I started to realize that these crises were just teaching me or preparing me to better know what I wanted to do, things started to come in baby steps. Then when I was ready for it, things just started to flow in at a faster rate. It was almost as if I got what I wanted when I was not paying attention to it or even cared about it anymore.

   My husband and I could not wait to get our first house and when we did, it was so exciting! However, it was not long before I realized this was not the house I wanted and it did not have all the details that I wanted in a home! It was not even in the location that I wanted! So I started making an even clearer and more detailed list of what I wanted, how I wanted it, and where I wanted it. I could see the house of my dreams in my mind, but was always reminded that it was a good thing we got this house first, because then I knew what I really wanted!

   What are some things in your life that you are grateful for that have taught you or helped you to realize what you really want? Please make a note on a separate piece of paper.

5) **Life is a test; it can make you BETTER or BITTER.**

   Boy, is this ever true for me. I have learned that you always have a choice how you want to look at life. *Everything* is a choice. To be happy or sad, to be bitter or glad, to worry or not, to be kind or unkind. We ALWAYS have a choice how we look at life. Your decisions really do determine your destiny, so choose wisely and positively.

   When I decided to quit my job due to circumstances that were causing me too much stress, I decided that I was going to look at it as a positive. This was just one door closing, and I was certain that another one would open soon. It was not easy (as I was treated very unfairly), but I tried really hard to not dislike my boss who made my circumstances physically and emotionally unbearable. Notice that I didn't say that I "hated "my boss...that was also a choice! Hatred is an extremely negative emotion that will just drain your energy, so it is best avoided altogether. I decided I was going to be better and not live a bitter life over it. This was a huge learning experience that required a lot of painful growth...but boy, did I grow!

Write about a painful situation in your life that you chose not to be bitter about, or if you were bitter, write about your plan on having a better outlook about it, because healing starts with how you choose to look at life. Please make a note on a separate piece of paper.

Andrea Lavallee is an Empowerment Awareness Consultant and Life Coach. She is the founder of The Empowerment Coaching Group, and the host of the International radio show, The Life Coach Radio Show, which broadcasts about connecting with Life Coaches and empowering the audience. Andrea is a Reiki Master Instructor, Certified Life Coach, NLP Certified Practitioner, Author, and Speaker. Andrea has a BA in psychology and had been empowering people for over fifteen years in the social services field before making to jump to Life Coaching and Reiki. Andrea is available for live speaking opportunities, in person workshops, and one-on-one coaching.

https://www.facebook.com/empowermentcoachingbyandrea

Alavallee2008@gmail.com

Empower Boost

Knowledge is Empowerment
by Amna Malik

What does empowerment mean to me? I believe that knowledge is empowering and liberating. Finding liberation through sound guidance by a teacher makes empowerment possible. As a teacher and mentor, I had the privilege and honor to work with students from various academic backgrounds, personalities, and interests. Observing students' reaching their learning curve at the end of a course has shown a remarkable state of realization and understanding of course materials. Reflection and confidence levels tended to soar and I could see students' level of enthusiasm, engagement, and conversations surrounding the relevance of research to practice. Knowledge ultimately became the epitome of empowerment; it provided students with the essential tools to translate research knowledge into health promotion programming, a career sought by many. It brought great delight and a feeling of accomplishment to witness such state, as is the feeling empowerment, by many.

How is empowerment aroused? As a wise Professor once said in class, "You cannot empower people, people empower themselves." As health professionals or advocates, we can guide an individual, a group, or community to realize and use their skill sets, strength, and provide them with tools such as knowledge and essential services to achieve their goals. I am currently working on an Adult Teaching and Learning Certificate to ensure that I have the necessary knowledge, and develop the skill set required, in designing and facilitating lectures, developing complimentary class activities, incorporating social media into lecture plans, performing evaluation and assessment using the appropriate method, and ensuring that my teaching style compliments a wide array of learning styles. As I take more courses, I feel more confident in my new skill set and understanding of adult education to improve my teaching style – I feel empowered.

What is the timeframe to feel empowered? Coming to a position of empowerment does not happen overnight, it's a process that takes place over time upon reflection. The knowledge and experience gained in a classroom setting, at work, traveling, through friends, or independent research materializes overtime into empowerment. I believe that empowerment has to transgress through the mind, body, and soul for it to settle into all our bodies, just as a plant becomes fruitful when provided with water, nutrients, and patience over time. Once can say that empowerment has to be nurtured.

As an example, I work with community groups to cultivate the land for communal garden programs. We perform all steps of the gardening process including the most fruitful step – harvesting. There is a feeling of accomplishment when you pick the food you have worked so hard for. Eating a healthy meal made out of fresh vegetables and herbs is even more than rewarding – it is empowering.

Amna Malik is a Health Communication and Marketing Professional, specializing in Nutrition, Health Promotion Programming, Adult Education, Research, and Community Development. Amna has worked and trained in many settings including University, College, Government, and Hospitals. She enjoys spending time with friends and family, and enjoys swing dancing.

Website: www.actnutrition.wix.com/eatwell

Empower Boost

Being One with Your Spirit
by Lori Canlas - De Pala M.S.W., R.S.W.

What is keeping you from living the life of your dreams? Most often we hear information of how to be physically and emotionally healthy, but what about your spirit?

The spirit is aware of the equilibrium; it regulates and warns of any possible imbalance that may prevent you from putting forth your best self. The spirit is an ever-flowing energy force that provides you with strength and vitality when your mind and emotions say you've had enough.

There is an infallible desire to feel you "have to be more" because you are "not good enough." When our minds, bodies, and spirits are out of alignment, we search aimlessly to fulfill ourselves by commercialism, addictions, busyness, and fame that would only momentarily provide temporal excitement and then catapult us into the sad reality of trying to keep up with standards of living beyond our means.

We can fuel our energy by tapping into the source of Higher Power, God, and the Universe (however, you address this power to be). It is giving yourself the gift of surrender although having experienced cruelty, shame, and guilt. It can be so haunting that it can weigh you down for a lifetime.

The spirit naturally searches for a calm, warm, and nurturing place to be satisfied. This very act of "spiritual alignment" is a form of prayer and meditation that captures our attention on how temporal our lives can be and how it can be snatched from our grasps at any point in time. However, we are vulnerable and this prompts us to search for God (higher power, the Source, etc.) so that we can be assured that we are not alone in this rigorous journey. These fragments are multiple crises that shape our hearts to move from external resources for satisfaction in life to seek spiritual fruits where our hunger "to be" can be fulfilled. What some may find is a tendency to turn away from God and blame God for all the losses, challenges, and hardships of life. Yet, these very challenges of life are cultivating the very depths of the heart and soul.

Knowing how to love deeply, by releasing ourselves from the attachment of the temporal and knowing that we are made to be whole, is our birthright! Nonetheless, once we are fully aware of the duality of our lives being in the midst of joy and sorrow, yet exuding an unshakeable peace and contentment of life, is extremely satisfying. Simply be with quietness of our souls in prayer and meditation.

Lori Canlas-De Pala is a Life Coach, a Registered Social Worker, has a Master's degree in Social Work, and is the founder of Bridging Dialogue Consulting. Lori's philosophy is "We cannot function to our fullest capacity until we have cared for ourselves. Caring for oneself allows us to fully care for others."

www.bridgingdialogueconsulting.ca

Chapter 30

Embracing Life's Lessons: 10 Tips to Live a More Empowered Life. Part 2

by Andrea Lavallee

6) **Transforming negative energies of anger and unforgiveness into understanding will create a much HAPPIER life.**

I learned this tip very early in my life. I have always had a natural ability to not dwell on the negatives in life. I understood that it does not benefit me to be angry, sad, or unhappy about people, things, or situations. When I see people feeling this way, it makes me dispirited and I want nothing more than to make them feel better about themselves and re-empower them.

But I also had to learn that not everyone wants your help. And that's okay – I can just focus on those who do. It is a very powerful thing to try to appreciate someone's situation, to see things from their point of view, and to understand. When you recognize their circumstances, then there is no judgment! But knowing that you don't need to help absolutely everyone is important too.

Have you ever experienced this? You meet someone, start to judge them, and maybe you listen to the negatives that people say about them. But then one day, you have an opportunity to know them better, and what you come to realize is that they're not the person you thought they were at all. In fact, you could have a lot in common and possibly become good friends.

Understanding does not create judgment. Understanding why someone does or says the things that they say and do creates non-judgment, so you are able to forgive and be happier.

My spouse and I are two different breeds. We are different in race, gender, culture, and religious systems, although we are both Christians. It used to frustrate me when he did and said some things that made zero sense to me. Once I tried to understand and not judge him (very hard when you are with someone for so long), it was totally worth it. I gained understanding and was much happier. Now, we laugh more. Love you honey.

In what ways can you come to understand someone more? If you gained understanding, write down what that was like for you. Please make a note on a separate piece of paper.

7) **Never Stop BELIEVING and never give up.**

Believing and not giving up was hard for me. Finding success and fulfillment in my career has been my greatest challenge…and greatest success. I tried so many things and ways to gain financial freedom, but just could not figure out how to do it. There's no network marketing that I have not tried, and failed at! It was all because I was not passionate about it; I only know that because I never gave up. I was very persistent. I kept trying and trying different things, always never giving up. It was painful and very disappointing many times, but I never gave up.

After thinking that something was wrong with me, I finally realized that I just needed to find a pursuit that I actually *enjoyed* doing, which turned out to be helping people through counseling and energy work. Once I decided that, I just needed to stick to that one thing and become very passionate about it if I wanted to start seeing results. It started off slowly, but as I put time and energy went into it, I began to achieve the outcome I had desired.

I remember getting down on my knees and praying a real and true heart-felt prayer of gratitude that I was able to finally be on the journey I was experiencing. But, I wanted to know where the results were. When will I get my reward? What would I do next? I had to stop focusing on the money and instead direct my attention on the real work of helping others, consistently having much faith and determination that I would get there, and never give up! I started to trust God more and more, and my faith grew a great deal through this. I turned away from putting my trust in mankind and instead put my trust in God. It was amazing! I started to gain courage that I never knew I had. My voice, which had been timid and tentative at first, gained confidence so I was able to speak on stage and connect to my clients with assurance and certainty. I have not reached all my goals yet, but I am not giving up!

Think of a time when you wanted to give up but did not, or what you learned from not believing or giving up. Please make a note on a separate piece of paper.

8) **Sometimes relationships can be WORTH working on, as long as they are not abusive (mental, emotional, physical, etc).**

Most of the time, we give up on relationships all too soon. We don't try to put the work into them to understand, learn, and grow from what is really going on. I always try to ask myself, "Is this hurting me or is it that my needs are just not being met?" Then all I need to do is communicate my needs or concerns.

Ask yourself, "What is the worst thing that could happen if I decided to talk about it?" Or be assertive, for example: "I don't like it when (_____), It makes me feel (_____)." I learned that if anyone made me feel inferior, it was because I allowed them to make me feel that way. The hardest thing to do is to take your power back, but it is also the most rewarding thing you can do to feel empowered.

After years of putting up with my mother's verbal abuse, I finally spoke up and said, *"When you talk to me like that, it makes me feel this way..."* She had a look of surprise on her face and I'm not sure if it's because I spoke up or that she actually had no clue what she was doing. Either way, I took my power back and ever since then, the energy between us has changed.

Think of a time when you needed the courage and speak up to get your power back. If you have not done that yet, think ahead of what you could and plan to say if it happens again. Please make a note on a separate piece of paper.

9) **We have WITHIN us the tools to seek help or get help.**

When you feel empowered and motivated, you will find that you are *full* of resources within yourself that you never even knew you had. I've had friends tell me that they've taken my advice before, even though I couldn't remember giving them the guidance! The words just come sometimes. Call it intuition or Spirit, but we all have this ability inside of us. We all have strength within, that when we are empowered and motivated, it comes out.

A friend of mine came in for Reiki and she had a lot going on that was weighing her down. She was in a state of transformation and didn't know what to do or where to go first. So, she started blaming. While she was on the table, I began coaching her and really connecting with her. I started to give her guidance, but because I was the person looking in, I was able to clearly see her strengths and the abilities that she herself could not see. I was able to give her the insight and direction that she needed to truly move on.

Think of a time when you were in that position and you were able to find within yourself resources or the necessary tools to help someone, or yourself, make a transformation. Please make a note on a separate piece of paper.

10) **YOUR life story is worth sharing; others will be empowered it. And don't be afraid to share!**

If you have a successful ending to a traumatic experience, then share it! If you have overcome the trial of your life, share it! Your experience can help so many individuals. People need constant inspiration and motivation. That is just how we manage to keep on going. There are too many things and people out there that are crushing dreams, so you need to be part of the counterbalance to that force.

Let's be the motivator, the one that inspires, the ones that empower!

Have you made up your mind to find your voice and own it?

Have you been awakened to the life you want to live?

Do you have a desire to empower others?

Are you ready to live your empowered life?

A really important part of my own story was my experience when I made the decision to take my life back and be in control of my destiny by quitting my job and finally living my empowered life. It wasn't the life that my friends and family wanted me to live, but rather the one that I wanted to live.

Don't be afraid – it's time you start living!

Andrea Lavallee is an Empowerment Awareness Consultant and Life Coach. She is the founder of The Empowerment Coaching Group, and the host of the International radio show, The Life Coach Radio Show. Andrea is available for live speaking opportunities, in person workshops, and one-on-one coaching.

https://www.facebook.com/empowermentcoachingbyandrea

Alavallee2008@gmail.com

Empower Boost

Divine Intervention or Law of Attraction?
by Andrea Lavallee

The Law of Attraction has become the most popular law and these days, we are overwhelmed by others telling us about universal laws. It is good to know that there are other laws and that some supersede others. For instant, the law of gravity supersedes the law of attraction. I realized that although I do strongly believe we are responsible for our outcomes and consequences based on our thoughts and actions, I started sensing that sometimes things just happen and that's just the way it is, as far as we can understand it. Here are a few reasons why I believe this is so:

1. Sometimes other people's choices affect how things turn out for us, but don't worry it's either a part of the lesson we need to learn or the consequences of their behavior towards us. It's nothing you have done to deserve or not deserve it.

2. There is a time and season for all things. We know that after Summer comes Fall. One did not cause the other; it's just the way it is. And it's the same in our own lives – we have our seasons where there is a time to sow and a time to reap what we have sown. Sometimes our sowing seasons are long and other times they are short. The things you have sown can take years to harvest. We just need to trust divine timing.

3. Sometimes you can try to manifest your dreams and goals and still nothing happens. This taught me that we are not on the right track. No matter how hard you try, it's just not in the plan of your

divine purpose. It's not your fault; you just need to figure out what is the next step for you.

4. We don't know what we don't know. There is more to life than we know and sometimes unpleasant things happen to good people. We can learn and teach from the pain. We usually don't try to manifest pain, it is just a part of the journey and the way it is.

Sometimes unexpected and undesired things just happen. Maybe you attracted it…or did you? There is one thing I do know and that is, no matter what occurs, there is always a divine purpose and a reason behind it. You just have to trust the process. Otherwise, you still need to set goals, think positively, have an abundant mindset, and work to build and accomplish your dreams and goals because that is what will guide you to find your true purpose, either by your own creation, divine intervention, or a combination of the two.

Andrea Lavallee is an Empowerment Awareness Consultant and Life Coach. She is the founder of The Empowerment Coaching Group, and the host of the International radio show, The Life Coach Radio Show. Andrea is available for live speaking opportunities, in person workshops, and one-on-one coaching.

https://www.facebook.com/empowermentcoachingbyandrea

Empower Boost

How the Internet Saved My Life
by Lisa Berry

It was my fifteenth attempt at trying to make a home in less than ten years. Maintaining any form of stability seemed impossible.

My life had become anorexic, carrying only a few bags as the weight I lugged around with me each move got lighter and lighter

You see, the less I had, the more I could control it, and the less I could lose and be hurt.

I slowly began to identify with "having nothing but myself," but it brought with it a dichotomy of enjoying the freedom while suffering and mourning each move as it felt like a death and failure.

Selfish, withdrawn, and scared, I pulled away from everything and yet was grasping onto anything. I needed to gain true control of my life to serve my highest self that I could sense was still in me, somewhere.

What helped me to harness that very sense, to nurture it, to grow it, what cracked through my darkness and shone the light on what would become my stable and trusted path, was actually the Internet.

Here I was, a published writer, a regular television guest and contributor, a solid holistic nutritionist, and life coach myself…and I was lonely, hopeless, and depressed.

I didn't see it coming. In one moment, one breakthrough…my life changed.

It was a hot summer day. I was sitting outside on a yoga mat on the grass with Brinx, my kitty, and my laptop, barely able to see the screen from the glare of the sun when I stumbled across a tele summit healing workshop. The guest speakers became my friends. They gave me hope and I began to speak of them as if they were by my side and existed in my real world. I needed them. I needed them to prove to myself that I had the courage; to demonstrate to myself and others that there was a better and glorious abundant way.

That summit not only led me to multiple other summits and Internet shows, but it saved my life and inspired me to do the same for others, which was my gift that already existed and I was hiding. The breakthrough was to see that "choice and responsibility for my highest self" was what I needed.

I have been almost three years now at the same address…confident, empowered, peaceful, and joy-filled. I'm able to support you in your journey of discovery and great transition!

Lisa Berry is an expert in breathing life into the dreams of those wanting to live vibrantly, energetically, happy, and fulfilled while standing confidently rooted in their personal power. As a Transitional Coach and Registered Holistic Nutritionist, Lisa recognizes her mission to find, help, and connect with those who want to shine.

lisa@datingyourdiet.ca

Chapter 31

Forging the Metal
by Lori Canlas - De Pala M.S.W., R.S.W.

Soot fills the dim air and multiple sparks fly from the luminescent iron rod as it is repeatedly pounded by the iron hammer. The blacksmith has greatly anticipated the formation in his mind of a sleek sharp edge, although the object that appeared before him was simply a blunt iron bar. His perseverance is tested by the unforgiving blaze that continues to cause him to perspire.

He slowly brushes his brow then braces his might as he draws back the heavily weighted iron hammer with his brawny arm and strikes the blade repeatedly and relentlessly as sparks from each blow scatters.

Empowerment is similar to the act of a blacksmith who rages against the elements to unveil a useful tool. Empowerment does not generously pour upon someone like a brash rainfall; rather, it is conscious and effortful work in very harsh working conditions. Similarly to blacksmithing, we are human; we are shaped by exposure to the elements that surround us. We anticipate the amount of effort and time it takes for a blacksmith to shape the iron. Forging the metal is likened to refining our own selves being shaped by the world that surrounds us.

My paternal lineage involves a string of blacksmiths inclusive of my father who knew of the harsh working conditions and hours it took to be refined at the art.

Nonetheless, it was my father who had chosen to change the course of his paternal heritage by refusing to be looked upon as just a blacksmith and an impoverished, uneducated young man. He yearned to be enthralled in a world of language and arithmetic. To his own father's dismay, he refused his fate to follow in the footsteps laid out for him to become the next family blacksmith; instead, he opted to pursue his own dreams of going to school and becoming a successful individual.

With his dream in mind and the willingness in his body, he longed to do what it took to make things happen for himself. He made a careful and calculated choice to leave the family home at a tender age of fourteen years, not knowing fully what the world outside of the home felt like. Although he was frightened, he was armed with a determination and fervor to follow his dream. He refused to be shoved in the category of have-nots and the relentless toil to work for his father, earning little money and having no freedom. It was a giant leap for him. However, he found that it was a small price for him to pay by leaving the family home. If he had stayed, he would have had to endure the criticisms from his father and the pangs of regret that he had to be without an education. He had an idea and dreamed of it. This was an opportunity to prove he was more than he could ever imagine himself to be.

Although he thought he escaped the criticisms of his father, he found himself confronting a new challenge. He had to deal with the teases and taunts of his relatives who cowered over him knowing he ran away from home when he was supposed to be the responsible eldest son of eight children. He did not know where he could stay, so he had opted to lodge with his relatives until he figured out a game plan of his own as his dream still burned brightly in his heart. He would do work around their home to help prove himself worthy. After all, since he was staying, he felt a strong need to demonstrate that he was not taking advantage of their hospitality. He believed the only way that he could gain the capacity to sustain himself was to be enrolled in a good educational institution. He had built his income the best way he knew how and it meant enduring working long hours with little pay. He went around asking others if he could work for them and he had convincingly informed them that he was willing to do the job. He had to prove himself trustworthy, although he did not have a resume or a great deal of work experience. All he was asking for was a chance, if they could allow him the space and time to prove to these potential employers his worthiness to entrust their most prized possessions with him.

A Haciendero (landowner) had willfully taken a chance on this eager young man because he had found that his workers were unable to keep up with their other responsibilities and take care of the stable. He wanted to have someone dedicated in taking care of the horses, and he felt my dad could be it. Although, my dad had no prior work experience taking care of horses, he was eager to learn on the job. He found himself working for the Haciendero and feeling like he was inching his way closer to going to school. He was enthralled at earning some money and would clean the stables, the horses, and talk to them as if they were human. He developed a love of horses and the horses developed a fondness for him too. There were days that he worked so hard that he didn't have a chance to go back home because it was too late and too dark to go. On those nights, he decided to lie on a stack of hay in the stables in order to get ready to work again the next day.

A few years later, he found himself looking for other opportunities. He found a tricycle company who had many drivers going out and about the local town and city. The tricycle is a motorcycle with a sidecar, a popular mode of transportation in parts of Asia including the Philippines. It is the size and cost of the tricycle that makes it a convenient and inexpensive way to get around. The manager of the company thought he could strike a deal with my dad and said to him, "If you work for me for a year and make a lot of trips, I will provide this very tricycle for you." My dad thought it was a great deal and gladly shook on it, while gleaming from ear to ear. This was yet another opportunity for him to earn his way to having an education. While driving the tricycle and picking up passengers, my dad completed his high school. Eventually, he became the proud owner of that tricycle.

After many trips and learning the back roads and the side roads of the local towns and city, he was able to earn enough money for his first-year university tuition. He enrolled in a Bachelor of Commerce program, and was able to study and hang out with the elite in his town. However, he saw how quickly the money had dwindled for that year and how many tricycle trips he would have to make to keep up with all the costs of his education. He came to the conclusion that it was not a sustainable option. He decided to go back home, visit his family of eight, and had a chance to see his younger siblings. When he saw them, he was moved and motivated to take action because he saw his former fate in them. My dad knew what would have happened to him if he had not made the outrageous choice to leave the family home in search for an opportunity to be educated. At that very moment, he vowed to them that he would earn enough money to help them go to school. They were ecstatic and looked upon him with much hope.

Sadly, he was unable to continue his studies in the Bachelor of Commerce program. He decided to continue driving the tricycle to earn enough money for his sisters and with the money left over, he would enroll in the Bachelor of Education program instead. Much to his parents' surprise and delight, he finished his Bachelor's in Education and became a teacher.

His sisters also earned their education and found meaningful work. He felt empowered that he could hang on to his dream with all his might and share it with his siblings. He creatively found ways to improve his well-being which forced him to mature beyond his young years. He envisioned the welfare of his family and furthermore, the prosperity of his community as he imparted knowledge to eager teenagers just like himself who hungered to be educated.

His defiance of the natural order and refusing to conform to the norm was actually exercising his ability to think outside of the box. By believing in a dream that had yet to become reality, he gave himself the willpower to obtain his internal right to vie on same playing field as his well-off counterparts. His desire was so strong that he had to challenge structures in his society that were powerfully pitted against him to achieve success. These odds against him were on many fronts: he came from a poor working-class family, he departed his home as a teenager, and left his responsibilities in the home, as the eldest son to take over the blacksmith business.

The impoverished notion that was embedded in society and the culture of that time was: if you were poor, your only fate was to remain poor. This very notion had controlled the mind of my dad's father. His father would preach to him that there was no point in trying to run after a dream because it would never happen, and would motion to my dad, using his arm extended a couple of feet above the ground saying, "This is where you are and this is where you will stay." The control of being ranked in a certain social class was carefully etched in the mind of my grandfather that it was passed on to my father. However, he had chosen to resist it. Therefore, his resistance ultimately changed the course of his life as well as his entire family.

Resistance is the notion to practice non-conformity when it is in the way of being able to achieve your life's passion. Although going against the grain is scary and may be ridden with the anxiety of a possible failed attempt, yet how would you know you can achieve greatness without giving your dream your best effort. When it comes to "who you ought to be in life," it is not going to be laid out for you. It will be up for you to search for it, define it, and do what it takes to unravel it in order to take ownership of your dream. Therefore, taking courage to stand up for what you believe in has to be stronger than the voices of those surrounding you who do not see your dream through your own eyes and how you would like to live.

The answer to your life's work is not dependent on the opinion of others, how you ought to dress, and what you have. We are fortunate and privileged to have choices; yet, we don't always recognize we have a choice of taking our lives to the next level. Not everything is set in stone and etched in silver. There isn't going to be a map or directions on how you can define your life's passion. It also takes resistance from the criticisms that may be haunting your own mind. It takes imagination, tenacity, and creativity to create your own map.

It means imagining a life for yourself that is inclusive of fulfilling your passion in life. It means not closely identifying with the way things are as they can be dauntingly enforced around you but it is by visualizing yourself grasping onto the idea of success that is not so farfetched, as it may seem.

My dad's longing to defy the odds in spite of hardship has stayed with me as one of my greatest life lessons. His life's journey, although is not so far-fetched from his beginnings as a child, is comparable to a dull piece of iron found in the dark corner. This piece of iron lies on the floor lifeless and cold. Yet once it is placed in the refining fire, it glows and is ready to be molded into its dreams. It will be shaped and fashioned as the Blacksmith envisions its final form. He toils and pounds through the iron; although he perspires, he powers through with excitement and anticipation. He forges the metal until he can see the resemblance of a blade. Then further he pounds on it, to be able to see it form. The blacksmith stands back in awe and affirmation. He wipes the blade with care and prestige as he sees yet another masterpiece that has been fully completed. He sees where life was breathed into this piece of iron, it has transformed into an instrument. Although he has endured a life's toil, sweat, and tears, his anticipated dream has become his lived reality where he looks back with joy and toasts a life well-lived and endured.

When Lori Canlas-De Pala was a young girl, she was in awe of the world around her. She remembers saying to her mother, "Today is special," who smiled back in agreement. Lori enjoys learning about connections people have once they've tapped into their realized strengths. This has compelled her to become a Social Worker because she wanted to know how people connect the dots of their lives. Lori loves to learn about what empowers people to be resilient during the most tumultuous adversities. Given this passion, she provides psychotherapy for adolescents, young adults, adults, and seniors.

www.bridgingdialogueconsulting.ca

1 (416) 707-2840

Empower Boost

I Made a Promise to Myself
by Andrea Lavallee

They say we chose our parents, in particular our moms. I figured if my son chose me to be his mom, then I needed to make a decision. The moment I was alone with him at the hospital, I made this promise: I would love him, have patience, and never be annoyed by him. Once I completed my thoughts, the most amazing feeling came over me: I was transformed. You see, growing up I was never very patient with kids and I definitely did not like rude or misbehaved ones. But this was also a reflection of how I grew up. I remember vowing to myself that my kids would never be disrespectful or misbehave. But the moment I saw his five little toes and his perfect little face, it didn't matter what he would be like. I just needed to love him. I promised I would be a patient and loving mother.

Over the years he has been the most loving human being I have ever had the pleasure to be in the presence of. He often would say the sweetest things. A few times as a family, we were looking at pictures, some of which were taken before he was born. We told him he was not in the pictures because he was in heaven waiting to come to us. He would say in his baby voice, "I missed you in heaven." Once I told him the doctor had to take him out of my tummy, he gave me a hug and asked, "Did it hurt?" His voice often sounded like an angel speaking. I was grateful to have him in my life because I had so much unconditional love for him and him for me.

As he grew up, I did all I could to understand him, his thoughts, why he had them, and why was he shy or anxious. I intended to help him live a happy life and to have a great childhood. I wanted to make sure he was the center of my universe. I was blessed when I started my business which allowed me to be around more often during his difficult times with his new school.

I needed to be his trusted friend and protector. He turned out to be a polite and well-behaved child after all. He has taught me how to love and to heal.

Andrea Lavallee is an Empowerment Awareness Consultant and Life Coach. She is the founder of The Empowerment Coaching Group, and the host of the International radio show, The Life Coach Radio Show. Andrea is available for live speaking opportunities, in person workshops, and one-on-one coaching.

https://www.facebook.com/empowermentcoachingbyandrea

Empower Boost

IQ_EQ2
by Barbara Finlay

What is more important in life? What you know or what you show? I was at a crossroads in my life and decided to put some energy into finding out about how others saw me.

I was already familiar with Personality Type Theory as I was certified to deliver some of the assessments myself. Among other things, I came across an IQ test online. I traveled to Toronto to write the tests to assess my IQ, and after a few weeks of waiting for the results, I received a letter inviting me to become a member of Mensa Canada.

I was relieved and a little sad. The "ah-ha" moment from this experience was that I now understood why I didn't really fit in – I always marched to the beat of a different drummer. It didn't really help me to plan a strategy.

The work that I did at a local agency was also important to me. It was while doing this work that I was asked to participate in supporting a group of adults that lived with the label of "developmental delay" to set up a self-advocacy group of their own. This is a population that rarely gets the opportunity to speak out for themselves. I attended a working retreat that was aimed at developing by-laws and policies to give a framework for their new organization.

I felt privileged to facilitate the discussions that weekend. As group members put forward their reasons for including or excluding some policies, they also included poignant examples and experiences that illustrated their positions. I was awestruck by what many of the individuals had endured and triumphed over. As we ended the weekend, I was approached by two members of the group who extended an invitation to be part of their organization. They explained that I "got" them; that I showed real respect for what they were doing. Well, of course I did respect their efforts and commitment.

I felt "in step" and honored to be asked to join this group; far more excited than I had been with the invitation to join Mensa. The IQ test was just filling in answers on a page, but the process I went through with this group opened up my intellect, heart, and soul. These people did not care what I knew, they saw in me a person who cared about what they wanted and was committed to helping them achieve their goals.

It did not matter how much I knew. It was more important that I showed others how much I cared.

I discovered that while IQ is just a number written on a page, EQ (emotional intelligence) is a whisper written on the heart.

Barbara Finlay has been a trainer and coach for twenty-five years. She currently assists small businesses and social enterprises with goal-setting and growth. Spiritual and personal growth are additional workshops topics and she enjoys hearing about the life journeys of others.

https://www.linkedin.com/in/barbara-finlay-758ba6b9

Chapter 32

I Knew It Would Get Better
by Laurentino Uscanga

I always knew I would become the person I was meant to be, despite being born into extreme poverty. Life was hard in the beginning, but it didn't deter me from becoming the man I am today. It has molded me into a better person and will make me a worthy husband and father one day.

It all started in Veracruz Mexico. There were the four of us: my parents, an older sister, and myself. Most times we could not afford clothes or shoes, and I certainly did not have many toys to play with. Being a boy, there were plenty of times when I wished I had a new toy truck or car. But I remember just making the best of it and always knowing in the back of my mind that things would get better.

Even then, I knew that there must be something better than being poor. I remember on the hill from our village was a community that did not seem poor and I recall wanting to be like them: having food to eat, shoes, or even a new toy. To have those things meant we were rich.

There must be something better than being poor. I also knew if I wanted to be like those living in the other community, I had to work hard for it, because hard work always rewards you. But even that would not be enough; I knew I had to work better and smarter.

I was not the best student in school, but I loved to study. Somehow, I did complete my college degree, where I studied Accounting. I also found out that even though I was shy, I was really good at debating and had a great understanding for politics. I later became a manager of over 100 participants at a boarding school. I started seeing the success I desired for myself.

Throughout my life, my family would put me down and compare me to my sister who had fairer skin and lighter hair. Even though I was often criticized by my family and others, I was finally finding success in life. But even with the little success I had gained I still felt like there must be something better. Although my family tried to lower my self-esteem by telling me I would never make it, I strongly believed there was more to me than just the limits my family had placed on me. I didn't want to be like them anymore – working hard but not getting very far in life. I could not see myself turning back to a life of poverty. My desire to become like the successful people on the hill made me want to try my hardest to become a better person.

By now, I was successful. I owned a car, I was the vice-president of a non-profit cooperation, I had a place to live, and was working towards my Master's degree. Like I said, I was always good at debating and I loved it, as I would often win first place for debating political issues while in school.

I was driven; I wanted to be better. I knew I needed to challenge myself for what I wanted, which was to leave Mexico and to come to a country with opportunities. So, for political reasons, I left Mexico and moved to the greatest country on the planet – Canada!

I arrived on December 9, 2004. I knew very little English and I only had $400.00 Canadian dollars in my pocket. I declared refugee claimant status and for four years, I lived in poverty again but all along I knew it was only temporary and that it was going to get better. While on welfare, I started educating myself in the English language and I learned to survive. After paying for my rent with the funds I was receiving on welfare, I had to subsist on $250.00 per month. After purchasing a transit pass for traveling, there wasn't much to live on. Thanks to food banks and other amazing resources, I had enough to live on, all along knowing my situation would not last. I never had any regrets because I was focused and determined to succeed. I didn't care that I was living in poverty, sleeping on the floor, not eating much or at all, or that I was struggling with the English language. I believed I would soon be living my dreams.

I learned English and lived this way for five years. The day I was granted citizenship (but not before being denied and having to appeal it), I remember it was the day of my freedom, the day I got the "green light" where I could access all the services available to citizens of Canada. Now I was free to get a better job, to vote, and to have all the rights of being

Canadian. But it was not over – I still had to get my career in order. I tried to get my Certified General Accounting assessed but found that I needed more courses. The problem however, was that I did not have the money for more training. I was eager to start my life and build a career in my new country, but there was this obstacle facing me, which was having the funds to get my information assessed. Life seemed hard again. What was I to do now? Would I have to put aside all my financial trainings and start over? I realized there is not much I could do but to change my focus for a more positive one.

Then one day I learned about a particular insurance and financial services company and that's when my life really started to change. Through them, I started to build my career in accounting and I was very happy. This company allowed me to do what I loved, which was working in finance without the high expense of taking courses. I understood I could get the exact same certifications as if I was taking a course I had to pay for. I also started training to do income taxes on my own.

Things only got better from there. While studying for my certifications, I started to work full-time in a warehouse and from there learned the ins and out of starting a successful recruiting business.

I was doing very well but there was something still missing. I was evolving and I needed to look for answers. I wanted to find out why? Why did my parents put me down? Why did my sister and then my girlfriend hurt me the way they did? They insulted me, took advantage of me, and treated me the way very disrespectfully. Why me? Why did I allow this to happen to myself? Why did I attract this? I wanted to learn more about human behavior. I wanted to find out how they could have done that?

I realized I had more to learn, so I found myself taking courses in social services at a Toronto area college. I remember presenting an assignment in front of the class where I had to talk about my family, and the memory of poverty came back and I cried like a baby in front of the entire class. It was a very emotional experience that allowed me to let go of so many of the feelings I was still holding on to. I was known as the guy who cried in class, but looking back, it was all worth it because I grew as a person. That single experience left me feeling a sense of forgiveness for myself and my family. Without this experience, I would still have bitterness and resentment about my upbringing. Now I am able to have a better relationship with my parents and family. It's not the best, but it's better than it was.

My message to you is, never stop believing in yourself. Know that you are better than you think you are. Don't let others tell you that you will never make it in life and never stop learning. Focus on what you want, assess where you are on your path, and if you are not closer to what you want for yourself, it means you are doing something wrong. Don't be afraid to go out there and find yourself. You never know what you will find or what will find you.

You should experience a shift every three to five years. If you don't notice a shift in your life, you are stuck and not growing. There needs to be constant growth.

These days, I am happier than I have ever been. I live in the best country in the world, I have found success in work and relationships, and I am very confident with who I am and where I am going. When I think about where I have been and how far I have come, I have no fear or doubt for where I am going or where I want to end up.

Life is beautiful. Live it with passion and it will treat you well.

Laurentino Uscanga was born in Veracruz, Mexico, but is now proud to call Canada home. He is enrolled as a Chartered Professional Account in the advanced level LLPQ license, a Primerica Financial Service District Leader with a Bachelor degree in Accounting, and a Social Service Worker Diploma from Fleming College. Laurentino considers himself a successful leader and sees himself as someone who never gives up on his goals. His motto is "Never stop learning." Laurentino enjoys spending time with family and friends, snowboarding, and traveling.

usla80@hotmail.com

Empower Boost

Money Matters
by Regina Neal

Most people have a strange relationship with money. They pursue it, work to earn it, and seek to find better ways to achieve more of it. Money plays a big part of our lives. They chase after money, but it seems to get away. When job hunting, they want the highest paying position. They work extra hours or second jobs to increase their income. They want the extra money because they think it will make them happier – more money to pay for the things they need for living and for the things they want to have or do. They try to save some money for the future, buy the things they need and want now, and hopefully leave some for the next generation. It is not the money we are after. Really, it is what money will get them, or at least they hope it will, such as, happiness, love, appreciation, significance, recognition, importance, etc.

Most of their lives, they chase after money, except for 4% of the population who work smarter and have money coming to them – no chasing. The trouble is not earning the money; the trouble is how much money is kept.

In 1983, my husband received a raise at work to $26,000. For the first time in my life, we were no longer poor. But, nothing changed; we still had the same attitude about money and the same spending habits as before. We were still broke from one paycheck to the next. This continued for years. The more we earned, the more we spent; not that we squandered it all, our living expenses went up, too. It seemed we couldn't get ahead. How do wealthy people do it? What is their secret?

For some wealthy people, there is no secret, they are just as broke, because they have the same bad habits: earn it and spend it. This is the money management system we learned as children. Although the income is higher, so are the expenses. Unless spending and saving habits change, the money problem will continue to exist at any financial level.

This was my problem until I learned about Money Blueprinting and the Easiest Money Management System. Now, I help others become wealthier using six bank accounts or six jars.

1. Don't spend everything you earn; save 10% from every dollar.

2. Pay yourself first. Save 10% and never spend it. This is your Golden Goose.

3. Money attracts money. You cannot attract money if your bank account is empty.

4. Give 10% to your favourite charities.

5. Your Fun/Play Money is 10%. Spend it, but stay in your limit.

6. Save 10% for Self-Education. Ignorance is far more expensive the cost of education.

7. Long Term Saving is 10%.

8. Learn to live within 50% of your income. Create a budget.

9. Know where your money is going. Keep a notebook. Record everything you spend.

Teach your children to do the same starting from their first dollar.

Do you want to reclaim control of your life, but don't know where to start? Meet Regina Neal, a personal development expert who specializes in attitude adjustments, taking you from "Victim to Victor!" Her mission is boosting confidence and courage for anyone facing stress, insecurity, and overwhelm with simple strategies to overcome.

www.youniquely.biz

Empower Boost

Relationship Tips
by Ana Marie Gonzales Agojo

Love with all your heart and accept the unlovable side of others, for anyone can love a rose, but only a great heart can include the thorns.

Every one of us wants to have a perfect relationship but nobody is perfect. In every relationship, there are so many problems that come and sometimes we don't know how we will solve them. It's four years and still counting that I'm in a relationship with the love of my life and I will share here the ingredients or tips that makes our relationship healthy, growing, and stronger.

We are believers of God. We always put God as a center of our relationship. And, we believe that a strong foundation in all aspects of our lives requires Almighty God. The relationship remains solid if you put God as a center of a relationship.

We are keeping our love alive. Although there are different things that make us happy, some of them may not have been on the list but should have been, while others are but should not have been. When all is said and done and the ink has dried up, all we really want is to love each other.

Being honest and have trust for each other must also be on a list. The most successful relationships are built upon trust, candor, and honesty; anything else is equivalent to building a house on quicksand. Receiving a pat on the back when we do things right is nice, but it is even nicer to be told when we're wrong, provided of course that we are not made to feel like crap; which takes us to the next point. We don't hide anything from each other. We express our feelings whether it is good or bad. We're honest about what we want about our relationship and what annoys us. Honesty is what holds the relationship together.

Another important ingredient in healthy relationship is respect. We're on May – December affair and age doesn't matter to us. We also have different cultures and traditions, but we accept our differences and love our similarities. Mutual respect is essential in our relationship.

We're always looking to get involved for the long haul, a kind of partner with a heart of gold, nurture and offer compassion, sincerity, warmth, and affection. We need to make it to the top. We are always affectionate and share the same goals in life. We express our feelings with each other, show that we care and how much we mean to each other.

We are in a long-distance relationship and we always keep connected. Communication is a key in part of any relationship. It's a common thread that binds us together.

Ana Marie Gonzales Agojo is a graduate of Bachelor of Science in Computer Science (Ladderized Program. She was born and raised in Batangas, Philippines along with two siblings. Ana Marie's passion for writing began at an early age in elementary school. She is now an aspiring entrepreneur.

agojoanamarie@yahoo.com

Chapter 33

The Blind Spot in the Bathroom Mirror

by Lisa Berry

Ohhh this was going to be bad. I already felt awful, embarrassed, kind of scared actually, but I couldn't even imagine how mom and dad were going to react or what they would do to me. I couldn't imagine any worse punishment than how badly I felt already.

I was a little girl, I had friends, a loving family, and I did well in school, but something made me lie to my best friend! I lied to feel that I was better than the other kids; I lied so that she would like me more than them. Looking back now, I can't even imagine how ego snuck in so quietly and quickly but it did and I fell victim to it.

What I thought was a harmless lie cause a domino effect, eventually leading to my best friend breaking her arm. I truly felt awful and was already deeply sorry, but I was also a kid who lied and there would be a punishment.

Mom often yelled at us girls. My sister and I were two regular siblings playfully poking at one another and testing each other's boundaries. Being separated for a time out, being sent to our rooms, and the occasional grounding wasn't uncommon but all disciplinary action made sense to me and probably secretly I appreciated mom stepping in to save me from our fights escalating. No matter what though, I always felt loved. But… back to my lie and the serious outcome. I remember feeling so awful that I wanted to be gone from the planet. Just vanish. I was terrified to face all the people and mostly ashamed to face my best friend.

The punishment was a shocker! It will sound very simple at first but I'll tell ya, it was the hardest and most life-changing punishment I ever went though. It became the foundation of how I was able to love myself deeply for the rest of my life.

Before I tell you what I endured, what I learned, and what I overcame, I want to ask you, "How do you spend time with yourself? How do you talk to yourself? How do you listen and hear what you think and want? What tone, what position do you take?"

I spoke of ego sneaking in at such an early age and I'm still shocked as my adult woman self thinks about this. I'd like to think that I knew myself as a child, and that I trusted and loved and thought highly of myself, but when I lied to make myself look better than the other kids, there was obviously a judgment I made about who I was. I wonder when that started, I wonder why I did, I wonder if we all do, and I wonder mostly how we all help each other to get to know our true selves and treat that self with kindness, love, and respect.

My mom knew how! This was my "punishment." The best punishment my parents ever gave me was a lesson on how to see what was in the blind spot of my own bathroom mirror.

A blind spot is defined as: an area where the view is obstructed, or where something is in the way, or where something is preventing or hindering a full view or deliberately making it difficult to see.

My mom first sat down with me on the edge of my bed, face-to-face, and looked me in the eye. Allow me to share that when you feel so ashamed of something you did, wow, is that uncomfortable. All I wanted to do was hide my face, feel loved and accepted, and erase everything. I'm laughing now but the weirdest thing was that mom was not yelling. This confused me even more. Mom went beyond asking me why I lied, because she knew not to stop at my confession that I wanted to look better than the other kids. She made me go deeper and asked why I wanted to look better than the other kids. Smart mom. I said I was scared that if the other kids were better than me, then my best friend would leave me and not be my friend. Mom explored this further and asked me if that did happen, did I not think I would make other friends? "Of course," as a little girl I replied, "I didn't want other friends. I wanted her as my best friend." My mom explored further and deeper and didn't leave either side of the coin unchecked. She questioned me from how I felt about the world, what I thought people felt, and how I felt about myself, giving me many scenarios to look at, think about, and reply to. Once this line of questioning was done, she told me to stand up. I was hoping this was the "big hug and all is well" part. It was not.

She told me to follow her. We left my room and crossed the hall to the bathroom where there was a full-length mirror on the door. She said I was to sit or stand in front of the mirror and have a conversation with myself, looking into my own eyes and at all my body parts. I was to understand, forgive, encourage, and love myself, all while looking in the mirror.

There were tears streaming down my mom's cheek as she directed me to do this. She said that it hurt her to know that the little girl she loved with all her heart didn't love herself as much.

The pain I saw, the compassion I felt for my mom as she exposed her wounds, somehow taught me right then and there what it felt like to be hurtful to one's self. She was in a way a mirror and in the reflection, I saw my value, my worth. If I wasn't valuable and if I wasn't worthy, this woman, my mother would not have such pain.

I stood there, in front of that mirror…shifting and fidgeting for a bit. Honestly, I was for sure thinking that mom was around the corner spying on me to make sure I was following through. But something happened. I sat down. I sat still. I looked in the mirror, and I looked through myself, to what I now call the "Blind Spot in My Bathroom Mirror." I started talking to the parts of me that had been hurt, sad, judgmental, angry, and even scared. I offered them loving words as I would to a best friend. It felt nice. I didn't feel lonely at all. I almost started feeling guilty for how great I felt and full of joy after doing something so awful. It was in that moment that I felt what forgiveness really was. My mom taught me how to know myself, how to forgive myself, and love myself in my perfect imperfection.

When I came to my mom after and asked if I could come out for dinner she said yes, but before that, there was one last part of the punishment/lesson. That was to phone my best friend and apologize to both her and her parents. Mom saw my face drop and shift with terror.

She said, "Lisa, there's no need for fear. Courage comes to you in difficult times when your strength is built on self-love and self-acceptance. You can now do anything."

Many of us stand in front of our bathroom mirrors and the blind spot can block different things for different people. For some, it's a complete avoidance as they ignore and numb all their pain and almost cower away from the beauty they deny. Other's blind spots are actually the love, the value, and the worth that they deliberately block and deny themselves as they allow the remaining part of the mirror to lie to them and only show disrespect and judgment. Most often, the bathroom mirror hears "you again, you're getting old, you are old, you're ugly, you better fix that, cover that, where did that come from," and the saddest "God I look terrible." But it's not just the mirror that hears that, it's you...it's your spirit, your soul, your heart, and your brain that hears this as well. You feel this. You start to become this.

I was one lucky kid to have had my mom make me check my blind spot. My ego still creeps in and when I hear and I know it's getting loud, I actually get myself in front of a mirror fast and I talk to myself. I have an honest conversation and explore what I'm feeling and then I follow that same exercise my mom had me do...understand, forgive, encourage, and love. I later found out about a Hawaiian forgiveness prayer called Ho'oponopono which has four very similar lines;

I'm Sorry

Please Forgive Me

I Love You

Thank You

For me as that little girl, my blind spot was fear that I wasn't good enough as I was, and fear that I'd be rejected or abandoned. There have been phases in my life when I haven't checked my blind spot and only saw what ego was reflecting back. Those were the times I wasn't standing in my true power and felt life was not at my fullest potential.

Now I make it a part of my lifestyle to check my blind spot and nourish the parts of me that need my acknowledgment, need my acceptance, and need my love. I have conversations with myself while looking into the mirror, into my eyes, and allow no shame to block or hide my light.

Look into a mirror, check your blind spot, and simply start by saying "I Love You, I accept you, deeply and completely."

Let the waters settle and you will see the moon and the stars mirrored in your own being... Rumi

Lisa Berry is an expert in breathing life into the dreams of those wanting to live vibrantly, energetically, happy, and fulfilled while standing confidently and strongly rooted in their personal power. She has turned up the natural light of hundreds of clients by helping them move from a place of trapped, scarred, or numb to a place of possibilities, choices, and feeling empowered to respond after listening to the hearts. Lisa fulfills her commitment as a Transitional Coach and Registered Holistic Nutritionist as she recognizes her mission to find, help, and connect with those who need and want to shine.

lisa@datingyourdiet.ca

1 (647) 449-4569

Empower Boost

Thank You Mum
by Janine Berridge-Paul

Living an empowered life is often challenging and takes time. Living an empowered life is not something that someone can teach you or give to you; it is something that needs to unfold naturally for you to experience it to the fullest. My life was once felt like the pain was never ending. The old me always believed that I was carrying the weight of the world on my shoulders. It would hold me back from happiness, success, and most importantly, from being my best self. I would only see the world through my pain. The story of my journey towards living an empowered life is filled with trial and error, tears and pain, but now I can stand here and say I have come such a long way.

I now fully feel each moment for the beauty and gift that it is and take life one day at a time. I stay away from being overwhelmed by the big picture and instead, stay thankful for the gift of every moment, every minute, every hour, and every day. Pain is in the past and I manage how I experience life right now. I have learned that I am in control of how I choose to feel, how I interpret my life experiences, who I surround myself with, how I react, and most importantly, I direct every step I take.

I thank my mother for helping me to reach this point in my life. Although she is no longer with me physically, I feel her guiding me through this journey every day. When I remember her and what she experienced, I feel empowered to live a happy and fulfilled life. She gave me the best life I could ask for and to watch hers be taken away too soon drives me every day to live the best way I can because I never know what the future holds.

Through her struggle, I admired her positive state of mind and how she always pushed through her adversities.

This is now how I choose to thrive. Her life set the stage for me to learn and adapt. Now no matter what life throws at me, I am aware that everything happens for a reason, which empowers me to always keep going. I embrace that my path is my own and I may not have all the answers. There is a power bigger than myself and I must keep moving the best way I know how. This is something we all can do and it will be unique to each of us.

Janine Berridge Paul's life path has truly opened her eyes and has shown her that the road to happiness and empowerment is in one's hands. Her experiences have allowed Janine to value her quiet time where she enjoys reflecting on life, love, creativity, and the beauty of imagination. She values giving back to the community through her work with youth and those involved in the justice system. Janine hopes to take her passions one step further by starting her own business and writing her own book. She is also a devoted wife and comes from a Caribbean family that is rich in culture.

Email: Berridge.janine@gmail.com

Empower Boost

The Biggest Mistake I Made in Business and How I Learned from It
by Allan Pollett

Back in 1999, I launched my first major online business: UCanBuyArt.com. I had a very "Field of Dreams" attitude to the internet at that time. I believed if you built it, visitors would come. After building and launching the site, I realized my mistake when the site had no visitors. To make things worse, the money used to build the site was my entire savings. With nothing left to market the site, I was in a difficult situation. But this was not my biggest mistake; it was deciding to try to sell original high-end art online.

At the time, the Internet was still relatively new and online purchases were not as common as they are today. People were nervous about whether they could trust paying via online transactions. Not only were people hesitant using their credit cards, but the normal way to buy fine art was to visit a bricks and mortar gallery. People needed to see the paintings before they felt comfortable enough spending $2000 or $3000. My site was completely an online shopping experience that offered only small 300 pixel wide images of the products. This was the time of early online services and dial up access, so I had to make sure the pages would load up quickly regardless of a person's internet connection.

So there I was in the worst possible situation: a web site, no visitors, selling things people weren't comfortable buying online, and at a time when people weren't ready to buy. I probably should also mention that I didn't know anything about art or know any artists willing to go on my web site. This online venture was a very big miscalculation. However, a few months later, I had over 300 artists, several million dollars in inventory, over

2000 visitors/day, and a few sales each month. What turned my horrible situation around was my natural talent for SEO and sheer determination. When I designed the site, I made each page target popular keywords and trained the artists on how to market themselves and the site. The site was able to make money and generate a modest income, but it was a major learning experience for me.

My take away from the experience: always budget as much for the marketing effort as you put into the web development costs. This is often the biggest oversight others make – they put everything into the development, but fail to realize that is only the beginning. Once the web site is built, the next step is to promote. Always understand your market and the demand for your product from the very beginning. When I plan to launch a new product or site, I check the Google's keyword planner tool to see how many searches there are for that product so I know what the demand is like. Also, I like at the top ranked sites and use SEMrush to determine how competitive they are, so that I will know how much effort is required to break into the market space. Ultimately, every mistake, even the biggest ones, can be beneficial as long as you learn from them and don't repeat them in the future.

Since 1998, Allan Pollett has been an SEO and web marketing specialist. He is known as the "SEO Guru" having written several books about reputation management, social media, and SEO related topics. Over the years, Allan has helped over 1000 businesses get to the top of the organic search results.

http://www.AllanPollett.com

Chapter 34

Having a Positive Fertility

by Andrea Lavallee

I would like to begin by sharing my story of how I became a fertility coach. Most people believe that when they're ready to try have a baby, it will happen quickly and easily. However, it does not come about that effortlessly for one out of every four women. So after trying to conceive my first child, I was surprised it took a year, but considering the fact that I was thirty-nine at the time, I thought I would go see a fertility specialist. I even requested a female thinking she would be more understanding. Well, it was not so. She confirmed that functionally based on my test results, everything was fine. My age was a factor, that must be the cause, and that was it. I had waited months to see the specialist and that was all she said. We kept trying and five months after that appointment, voila! We conceived. My son is now eight years old and was worth the wait. We weren't really trying to have another baby when I conceived my second child. But, eleven weeks later, I miscarried. It was very heart-breaking because I was now forty-two and figured we lost our last chance of conceiving a sibling for our son. I went to see my Gynecologist and all he had to say was, "Well you are running out of time." Very text book and not very comforting. During this journey, I have discovered what I would like to call Positive Fertility. What does it mean, you ask? It's something I felt can help many women out there trying to conceive.

During my time as a Fertility coach, I have created the following program, which I called the Conception System.

FORGIVNESS – I know how it feels to experience defeat, hopelessness, and uncertainty about your fertility when month after month there's no success. But I also understand what it's like to get that success, so my mission is to tell you to never give up hope. Trust me – there is a spirit baby waiting to come to you, but sometimes it's up to us.

Forgiveness – When you don't forgive yourself month after month, the more money that is spent on your fertility with no results, and months and years go by and still no outcome, you are bound to feel that you are doing something wrong and may even start to blame yourself or your partner. But I am here to tell you that not having forgiveness for yourself and the burden that it carries, creates blocks in your energy field and could delay conception. So, you need to work on forgiving yourself, find a way to prevent this turning into a stressful time, because studies are now showing that stress does delay conception – even low levels of stress can have an impact of your fertility. You need to ask yourself what it feels like when you blame yourself and are not very forgiving. Do you become emotional, do you shut down, and don't want to talk to anyone? Depressed? Ask for feedback.

There are four tools you can use to help be more forgiving of yourself.

1. First thing you will need to do is develop **COPING SKILLS**. My ebook *"101 Things to Consider on Day 1 of Your Cycle When You Are Trying to Conceive"* is filled with coping skills. Things you can consider doing so that you don't become despair – some of the things discussed are one of my favorite – get excited about ovulation. Just because you were not successful that month, it's not the end. Look at it as the beginning, that way it's called Day One. Get excited about when you will ovulate again. This will help start your cycle on a positive note. It's okay to be sad. It seems like the end, but don't be sad for long. Turn it around and get excited again for another opportunity.

2. Another tool is to start a **BABY JOURNAL**. Don't look at the start of having a relationship with your baby when its born or when its conceived, start having a relationship now. Write all your thoughts and dreams in your baby journal. Write about how you were sad today because you can't wait for him/her to come into your life, because you're looking forward to loving and caring for him/her. Journal writing is a great way to forgive yourself and relieve stress.

3. Next, **AFFIRMATION**. Affirmations are a great way to lift your spirits and find yourself back into the light. Some sample

affirmations are:

- I am in the process of having a healthy pregnancy that will bring a baby into our lives.

- I am healthy and strong and am able to conceive a baby.

- I am happily preparing to be a great mother/family.

- I am in the process of preparing my body to conceive, to carry, and to give birth to a healthy baby.

4. Try **MEDITATION**. Visualize your baby coming to you and finding joy in that day when you will hold it, smell it, kiss it.

All of these tools will bring much relief in knowing that you are doing all that you can to bring this spirit into your life, including reducing your stress.

TRUST – I need you to know I am referring to Trusting yourself. We all know the we have a cross to bear, and what I mean by that is some people suffer from chronic pain, some struggle with mental health, some have financial issues, and some infertility. Don't look at infertility as a disease, rather it's the cross you're called to bear right now. Put that intention out there to the Universe so that you can get some understanding around it. Ever since I can remember, I always look at this on a spiritual level and teach from the spiritual. So I considered my experience as a lesson that I needed to learn about my spirit baby. I want you to say, "I have a spirit baby." At the end of the day, you need to trust this process that you are on. You need to believe that everything will work out the way they're supposed to if you believe it. If you trust that you are on the right path about your fertility, then you are. This is why the spirit baby chose you because it wants you to have this experience; it wants to come into the world this way. This IS the way it is meant to be for you.

CONCEPTION CRADLE – The foundation of my fertility coaching is based on my understanding about spirit babies. This concept is based on the following: when you and your partner are intimate and are creating a baby, something magical happens – something you cannot see. It all starts with the energy called kundalini. This energy starts at our root chakra and is the energy of creation. When it flows through your chakra system, it becomes a powerful force that transforms your life physically, mentally, and spiritually. Kundalini begins to run through your energy systems when it is time to create a new identity. It is stimulated by life-transforming actions or desires. Meditation practice, sexual activity, and a conscious or unconscious desire to have a child are some examples of the wide range of kundalini stimulants. Once kundalini begins to run through your system, you feel imbued with the power of creation. You are willing to sacrifice and totally transform your life in order to achieve your goal. When couples with a conscious or unconscious desire to have a child make love, their kundalini energies flow up their spine and out the top of their heads. Their individual energies intertwine, forming a column. At the top of the two energies merge into the shape of a bowl. The whole form resembles a large gold and orange goblet or chalice. The conception cradle floats above the top of the prospective mother's head, and calls and welcomes the spirit baby. Safe in the conception cradle, the spirit crosses over from the world of spirits and makes first contract with its new body. If the spirit baby accepts the new body, the fertilized egg will successfully plant itself in the mother's womb. This process is called Conscious Conception, meaning actively participating in the process of creating a child. Conception is both a physical and a spiritual union through sperm and egg; they also commit a portion of their vital life force, or Kundalini, to this act of creation. So next time you are in the process of creating, I want you to visualize both your energies intertwining and forming a cradle and glowing a brilliant gold and orange bowl above the mothers head calling your baby.

Just as there are physical problems that can inhibit the joining of sperm and egg, there are also energy blocks that prevent a viable conception cradle from being formed. In these cases, practicing conscious conception can dissolve these energy blocks and helps open the door to conception.

So there you have it. I really wanted to share these tidbits with you because I know there are people who could really benefit from this. Sometimes it just takes a small change to make a big difference.

Andrea Lavallee is an Empowerment Awareness Consultant and Life Coach. She is the founder of The Empowerment Coaching Group, and the host of the International radio show, The Life Coach Radio Show. Andrea is available for live speaking opportunities, in person workshops, and one-on-one coaching.

https://www.facebook.com/empowermentcoachingbyandrea

Alavallee2008@gmail.com

Empower Boost

This Wasn't Part of My Plan
by Michelle Carter

For as long as I can remember, I had one dream and one plan: to be a professional singer and only a singer! I had my plan all mapped out. I would be plucked from obscurity, get a record deal, and tour the world! And that was that. EASY!

I studied classically, then went to music school and did everything "right." I joined a band, where we wrote and recorded amazing music, and received tons of accolades. But then that fell through after six years due to a tragic event just as things were taking off in a major way. This was like a death - it was the spoke in the wheel of my plans. "This isn't the way it supposed to happen," I would tell myself. "This wasn't part of my plan."

So "not part of my plan" became the story of my life. I felt as if I had lost my identity. Who was I if I wasn't a singer in this band? It was devastating at the time because I had to reinvent "the plan." I got annoyed with one too many guitar players, so I learned to play guitar myself. I got hired to play keys for a gig, so I learned piano as well. I got hired to do some songs for commercials, so I got a home studio and learned to produce. All the things that I relied so heavily on others before, through all the upsets and "failures" I had acquired all these new skills. Now I do sing every day and I also have created a little world of my own opportunities! Had everything worked out as smoothly as I had planned... I would be just be a singer.

I love that my work is to create music and when I let go of what it was supposed to look like, all sorts of strange yet wonderful opportunities just presented themselves. When I look at my own life, I realized how much pain I caused myself from strangle-holding that one plan. When it felt like rock bottom and I really, truly let go to what's possible, my whole world changed!

Today I still have HUGE dreams but I am very open to how I get there. Everything is possible! All the pain and all the mishaps were totally worth it because I am stronger today, personally and musically. I just know the road that I took was my road and not to compare but rather be inspired and know we are all so different. We don't know the plot twist or the ending yet…isn't that more exciting? My advice is to stay in your DREAM and be flexible with your plan!

Michelle Carter is a classically trained singer/songwriter/composer based in Los Angeles. She uses contemporary and traditional instruments to craft her unique sound. She spends her days in LA composing music for film and TV. Michelle has been immersed in spirituality and self-development, sound healing, and alternative therapies, progressed naturally from a very young age.

www.michellecartermusic.com

Empower Boost

Tools to Maintain Emotional Wellness
by Andrea Lavallee

Just when you feel like you've had enough - dealing with your less than understanding sibling, parent, friend, or boss - you can choose to take it, or not. Very few people know how to be assertive and stand up for themselves. If this sounds like you, then this empower booster is for you.

If you decide to not be subjected to that behavior any longer, then take a deep breath, close your eyes, and tell yourself, "That's it! I am done being a door mat. I am done playing victim and I am going to do something about it."

Here are a few tools I have used in my "Plan of Happiness" workshop that has helped participants to gain control and move forward to finding some peace.

1. Burn it - You can write your "pain" on a piece of paper and burn it, rip it up, or flush it. The idea is that once you're ready to move on from the distress, this is a symbolic way to get rid of the issues holding you back from living your empowered life.

2. Prayer - When you pray, you are raising your vibration, which is shifting your life, meaning that you are already making a change for the better. Don't forget to ask for help when you pray. God will help those who help themselves. Don't say that you don't have to ask. He knows what you need; of course this is true. He does know, but He is giving you the choice to ask for help.

3. Grounding - This is very simple. All you have to do is use the power of your mind and visualize your feet planted to the ground. It could be as simple as roots coming out of the bottom of your feet and going into the ground as deep as you can imagine. This is a very empowering way to hold firm especially if you want to feel stronger around someone who drains your energy.

4. Gratitude - This one is very straightforward yet very profound. You can start by keeping a gratitude journal and every night write down all the things you are grateful for.

5. Visualization - You can have so much fun with this. You just visualize your goals. As you do this, the universe is serving up the order. Have you all heard the saying "What you focus on expands?" Make a list, then visualize your dreams and goals, but be careful because you can not hesitate. Be sure you know exactly what you want without any doubts, fears, or wavering.

So there you have it. Five simple tools to help you improve your life and manifest your dreams.

Andrea Lavallee is an Empowerment Awareness Consultant and Life Coach. She is the founder of The Empowerment Coaching Group, and the host of the International radio show, The Life Coach Radio Show. Andrea is available for live speaking opportunities, in person workshops, and one-on-one coaching.

https://www.facebook.com/empowermentcoachingbyandrea

CONCLUSION

Well, there you have it. How do you feel now that you have read these powerful stories of hope and determination? I trust I have accomplished my goal which is for you to feel empowered and to have realized that if the co-authors can do it, you can too. If they can pick themselves up again and again and preserve, then you can as well. If they're able look at the world through rose-colored glasses, then you definitely can too.

Feeling empowered to not be fearful of the hard work and courage that will get you to finally say "No more!" and to find it within yourself to live your best life is my intention. So I ask you "Who inspired you the most? Who did you feel a connection with? Who made you say, 'Wow, it's like he or she is talking to me?'" If you have that feeling of connection and inspiration with any of the co-authors, then feel free to send them a message of gratitude. It takes courage for someone to tell their story and I'm sure they would love to hear from you about how much their story touched you.

Finally, I hope this book has inspired you in a holistic way – mind, body, and soul. Physically, to make a change for a better you; Spiritually, to raise your vibration to become a more evolved person; Emotionally, to find the strength that has been hidden for so long (it got buried by many years of fears); Mentally, to know when you finally have the courage to say "I am ready to Keep Calm and Live my Empowered Life."

Andrea Lavallee

Andrea is an Empowerment Awareness Consultant and Coach. She is the founder of The Empowerment Coaching Group and the host of the international radio show, *The Life Coach Show*. Andrea is available for live speaking opportunities, in person workshops, and one-on-one coaching.

Closing Remarks

Thank you for reading our beautiful book. It is my greatest desire that you have been enlightened with the essence of what it takes to be a Soulful individual filled with Love & Empowerment, and what it really means to that powerful and courageous soul.

This is a highly sought-after book and is successful because of all the contributors sharing their own ways of finding empowerment and appreciating the various kinds of love there are to achieve the life we all seek, despite dreams that were broken, lost, or stolen from their lives at their most susceptible times. It has given each author a life full of unlimited potential and triumph. Also, by choosing to have an attitude of love and empowerment, it has helped many to attract a life of satisfaction and gratitude. They refused to remain emotionally stuck in negative or even damaging situations.

My intention of publishing these self-healing books is to inspire you to reassess your own life experiences with an enlightened perspective. You are never alone in your journey. With so many stories of love and empowering perspectives revealed in this book, it would be something to see how we can all change the world with just a little more love, peace, and unity, one woman, man and child at a time. I encourage you to give up the things that have hurt you or held you back. Give yourself the authorization you need and let go of your own individual confines within your soul, as you continue to ponder the wisdom and life experiences of all our contributions. We have all eagerly permitted you into our world regardless of how painful and hurt our feelings have been through various experiences that ultimately led us to find the hope we needed to carry on.

The wealth that is within this book is eternal. As gold never loses its value, the many perspectives of what self-healing means to you will always hold its personal value, just as each heart-felt emotion was poured into each chapter. This kind of insight alone is enormous and worthy of examination and application in one's day-to-day life.

As the CEO, Founder, and Publisher of LWL PUBLISHING HOUSE, I have supported and mentored all my clients successfully and would love to help you also become a Best-Selling author. In doing so I have managed, coached, and organized several groups of international Best-Selling co-authors in the last three to four years, and have now published this tenth anthology. That's 330 people from around the world who are now recognized as leaders and experts among their peers, as they choose to step into their own achievement and recognition!

Now, my question to you is: "Do you have a dream of writing your own beautiful book? Do you want to inspire, motivate, and encourage others? Do you feel your story and vision can help others to live a life without limiting beliefs and roadblocks in their own lives? Have you gone through something that is so incredible and know that many need to hear your story?" I would be honored to guide and coach you into compiling and writing your own life-changing anthology if you are a visionary that believes in yourself, but just need that professional direction to pull it all together. What are you waiting for? Contact me and let's discuss what your next steps would be to become one of LWL PUBLISHING HOUSE's newest International Compilers.

My company is offering incredible single author packages as well as Children's book authoring opportunities through LWL KIDz. Our Best-Selling books are listed within the categories of self-help, healing, relationships, faith, and positive psychology to name a few.

I would love to help you organize, manage and publish your book project, as it's also considered an entrepreneurial success step to brand building your business through a book.

I have learned so much about people and what makes them inspired and motivated from twelve years of specialized experience as a Registered Nurse and almost twenty years in health care, as well as my extensive training to become a Certified Professional Coach, Living Without Limitations Conference Host and Founder, and of course Best-Seller Publisher, just to name a few.

I understand the frustrations and stress of trying to write your own book. My professional LWL Support Team and I want to assist you in making your dreams and goals a reality as a published author and I want to show you how to do it as quickly as possible. Together we will develop a "Master Plan template for your publishing success." Our goal at LWL PUBLISHING HOUSE is about bringing your vison to life in print.

Anita Sechesky

CEO of Anita Sechesky – Living Without Limitations Inc.,

Founder and Publisher of LWL PUBLISHING HOUSE a Division of Anita Sechesky – Living Without Limitations Inc.

Best-Seller Mentor, Book Writing Coach, Registered Nurse, Certified Professional Coach, Master NLPP and LOA Practitioner, multiple International Best-Selling Author, Workshop Facilitator & Trainer, Conference Host, Keynote Speaker.

Join Anita's Private Facebook group: LIVING WITHOUT LIMITATIONS LIFESTYLE. With over 960 members, she offers exclusive prizes, co-authoring opportunities, Random Contests with FREE Publishing possibilities, "Inspired to Write" Webinar classes, and more - http://bit.ly/1TlsTSm

Please visit Anita's Facebook page: LWL PUBLISHING HOUSE

Website: www.lwlpublishinghouse.com

Email: lwlclienthelp@gmail.com

Join Anita's Private Facebook group:

LIVING WITHOUT LIMITATIONS LIFESTYLE: Exclusive prizes, co-authoring opportunities and Random Contests with FREE Publishing opportunities. - http://bit.ly/1TlsTSm

YouTube Channel: http://bit.ly/1VEGHew

Website: www.anitasechesky.com

LinkedIn: https://ca.linkedin.com/in/asechesky

Twitter: https://twitter.com/nursie4u

LWL PUBLISHING HOUSE

Available on all Amazon sites.
http://amzn.to/2rszwKO

LWL PUBLISHING HOUSE

Available on all Amazon sites.
http://amzn.to/2mQHY6A

LWL PUBLISHING HOUSE

Available on all Amazon sites.
http://amzn.to/2mQWWtk

Soulful Stories of Love & Empowerment

LWL PUBLISHING HOUSE

Soulful Stories of Love & Empowerment

LWL PUBLISHING HOUSE

Soulful Stories of Love & Empowerment

LWL PUBLISHING HOUSE

www.ingramcontent.com/pod-product-compliance
Lightning Source LLC
Chambersburg PA
CBHW070054080526
44586CB00013B/1050